FRANCIS AND RIVY, AUGUST 1914.

Francis and Riversdale Grenfell

A Memoir

BY

JOHN BUCHAN

THOMAS NELSON AND SONS, Ltd.

LONDON, EDINBURGH, PARIS, AND NEW YORK

First Published October 1920
Second Edition, November 1920

I SHOULD like to dedicate this little book to the
Twins' brothers and sisters : especially to their sister
Dolores, who was rarely absent from their thoughts
—or they from hers.   J. B.

Degno è che dov'è l'un l'altro s'induca
Si, che com' elli ad una militaro,
Cosi la gloria loro insieme luca.

DANTE, *Paradiso*, xii., 34–36.

Ah, that Sir Humphry Gilbert should be dead :
Ah, that Sir Philip Sidney should be dead :
Ah, that Sir William Sackeuill should be dead :
Ah, that Sir Richard Grenuile should be dead :
Ah, that brave Walter Deuoreux should be dead :
Ah, that the Flowre of Knighthood should be dead,
Which, maugre deadlyest Deathes, and stonyest Stones,
That coouer worthiest worth, shall neuer dy.

GABRIEL HARVEY, 1592.

CONTENTS

ILLUSTRATIONS

PREFACE.

BY FIELD-MARSHAL LORD GRENFELL, G.C.B., G.C.M.G.

THE Twins wrote to each other almost daily, and
when Francis went to the Boer War they settled
to keep each other's letters. A large collection
was found after their death, and when examined
it seemed to their family worthy of some form of
publication. Mr. John Buchan, who was one of
the Twins' greatest friends, most kindly undertook
to prepare a memoir. It is intended that any
profits derived from the sale of the book should
go to benefit the finances of the Invalid Children's
Aid Association, a branch of which was founded
in Islington by Rivy in 1912, and in which both
brothers were greatly interested.

On September 5, 1880, when quartered at
Shorncliffe, I received a telegram from my brother
announcing the birth of the Twins. Thus the
family of seven sons and four daughters had
increased to a total of thirteen. Of these, eight
went to Eton, four of them being in the Eleven;

one entered the Royal Navy, and five of them died in the service of their country—Pascoe, the eldest, killed in the Matabele rising ; Robert, 12th Lancers, my A.D.C. in Cairo, in the charge of the 21st Lancers at Omdurman ; Reginald, 17th Lancers, of illness caused by service in India ; Francis and Rivy in the Great War. All the surviving brothers served in the war, one as Brigadier-General, and three as Lieutenant-Colonels.

My various military appointments and duties kept me out of England most of the time the Twins were children and boys at school ; but on the death of their father, when they were sixteen, I became their guardian, and our friendly relations of uncle and nephew became much more intimate and more like those of father and son. I was known to them as " The Uncle," and was accustomed frequently to hear the phrase, " Go it, Uncle."

I remember arriving on a visit to them at Eton and finding their room strewn with answers to their appeal for help to build new kennels for the beagles, of which Francis was master. They were then at the zenith of their popularity and success : Francis in the Eleven and Master of the Beagles, Rivy Whip, and both members of Pop ; and I felt my position as Sirdar of the Egyptian army to be a far inferior one to that of my nephews at Eton.

Later, at a review of a large number of Public School Cadets by the Queen, I, in my official capacity, was standing close to Her Majesty to announce the names of the various schools, when the leading company of Eton Cadets marched past, and I was alarmed to hear the usual signal whistle of the Twins to me, with the exclamation " Hullo, Uncle ! "

Francis was my godson, and began his military career in my regiment. When staying with me as extra A.D.C. at Malta he received his commission in the King's Royal Rifles in 1901.

The visit of the Twins to Malta had a decided effect on their future. They met interesting men of the army and navy, and began to realize the vast extent of the British Empire, and also their own ignorance of its history and geography. They had never even heard of Napoleon III. and the last French Empire! Our daily readings, especially the *History of Our Own Times*, enlarged their understandings and made them eager for further instruction and more knowledge. From that time dates the remarkable assiduity with which they pursued their studies, both in languages and history, especially military history, and laid themselves out to meet men of culture and distinction, whose acquaintanceship they felt would be useful in the future.

Each was invariably in the other's mind, and they sometimes had premonitions of harm. When Francis fell ill at Inverness with what seemed at first only a chill, Rivy, who was staying with me, said he *must* go to Francis. Oddly enough he was quite right, as when he arrived in Scotland he found him very ill with typhoid fever, no telegram or warning having arrived.

Rivy settled down to a financial career, and when travelling in America he studied the management of railways and methods of business. While there he astonished a friend of his father's by asking him if, as a favour, he might work in his office next to one of his clerks. " Why, certainly you may," was Mr. Morton's answer. " I am an old man, and have often been asked for a holiday, but this is the first time any man enjoying a holiday has asked me for leave to work."

While taking their occupations seriously, as companions they were most cheerful and humorous, original and quaint in their points of view, and very amusing in the simplicity of their observations. Many were the instances of their sympathy and kindness to others. Francis on one occasion sat up all night with a porter at the Bath Club who had smashed his hand in an accident, and this was at a time when he was preparing for an important examination. Happy days were spent at Butler's Court, which was open to them and their ponies whenever they cared to stay, and I was much struck by the efficient management of their stud. Their affection for my children, shown in so many ways, was a delight to me and to their mother, and the attention shown to the villagers and old employees of Wilton Park made them very popular.

As children they had adopted Lord Burnham, who lived close by at Hall Barn, as a most intimate friend. He was much amused on one occasion when they stayed with him during the holidays for a ball, and appeared wearing large pairs of white gloves borrowed from the footmen, whose billycock hats they also wore in church the next day. After Francis's death Lord Burnham wrote a most beautiful and touching leading article in the *Daily Telegraph*. They were devoted to him and his family, and their affection was reciprocated.

The Twins sympathized with all in sickness or sorrow; and in the greatest affliction that can happen to any man, they arrived to stay with me and made themselves most useful and helpful.

In 1901 Francis began his military career in the King's Royal Rifles. The strong wish to join the cavalry, which I think had always been in his mind (three of his brothers having been in cavalry regiments and two in the yeomanry), could not be carried out at that time for financial reasons; but this was an abiding desire, which the attractions of so good a regiment as the King's Royal Rifles did not quite eradicate. He did well in the regiment, and on his death the colour-sergeant of his company wrote to me to say what an efficient company officer he had been, and what care he had taken in the instruction of the men. One reason why he desired to transfer from the infantry to the cavalry was that the effects of enteric still clung to him, and he found the long route marches of the infantry almost unbearable. But he always acknowledged that his short service in the King's Royal Rifles had greatly assisted him in his career, and that he acquired there the soldier-like qualities of training and discipline.

On his return to England in 1907 we saw a good deal more of each other, and it was delightful to see his happiness in the cavalry, and his determination to master all obstacles which would prevent him from joining the Staff College. I had the opportunity then of reading his criticisms and notes on manœuvres, which were excellent and commended in the regiment. In my opinion he would have eventually taken a high place in the army as a cavalry leader. He loved his squadron and his regiment, and he left no stone unturned to fit himself for eventual promotion and command.

A course at the Cavalry School at Netheravon, and several visits to his friend Colonel Félines at the French Cavalry Establishment at Saumur, together with his attendance both at French and German manœuvres, show by his voluminous notebooks that he had taken the greatest trouble thoroughly to study cavalry training, tactics, and command.

He possessed the highest ideals of discipline in the conduct of war, tempered by a happy power of commanding the affection and obedience of men, especially of his own squadron. His desire for knowledge was insatiable, and he used every endeavour to achieve his objects. I remember, quite in the early days, finding Rivy and Francis in their small room at the Bath Club, notebooks in hand, and Dr. Miller Maguire lecturing to them on military history with all the care which he would have bestowed on an audience in the United Service Institution.

On the 30th August, after the first month of war, I found Francis at No. 17 Belgrave Square, the temporary and well-appointed hospital of Mr. Pandeli Ralli, where I told him that he had been recommended for the Victoria Cross. He received my news with surprise and said, "This honour is not for me—my squadron gained it"; but he was greatly pleased when Lord Roberts and Lord Grey came to congratulate him.

When able to move he came down to me at Overstone, and there I had the sad task of breaking to him the news of Rivy's death. His brother Harold, whose brigade was being inspected by the King that morning, was taken aside by his Majesty and told that Rivy's name was mentioned among the casualties, and he came right away to Overstone to tell me. Francis received the news quite calmly, but from that moment he was a changed man in everything but his enthusiasm for his regiment and his desire to get back to the fighting line.

His Majesty showed gracious and kindly interest in both, and gave Francis a special interview, the account of which I quote from his diary :—

"On Monday, February 22, 1915, I was ordered to go to Buckingham Palace to receive my Victoria Cross, driving there in khaki with my sister. Was shown into Clive Wigram's room, who told me of the heavy loss of the 16th Lancers. A few minutes before eleven we went into the equerry's room, and he took me upstairs to the King's room, which I entered. He was alone in the room, which looked like a study, with many

Indian ornaments about. The King came forward and shook hands with me. As my right hand was wounded, I was only able to use my left. Both remained standing and talked for some time about the war. He had heard of the heavy loss of the 16th Lancers, and that we had been sending out some 15-inch howitzer guns which would greatly strengthen us, and every day we were getting stronger. I asked the King if he had visited the prisoners who had come from Germany. He said he had, and described how badly some of them had been treated, and spoke strongly against the Germans. He then stepped back and took my Victoria Cross out of a small box and pinned it on to me, congratulating me on getting it. He said how sorry he was for the loss of my twin brother. I said I had not deserved the Victoria Cross, and hoped he would allow me to convey to the men who really deserved it his kind congratulations and good wishes. I said I hoped in the future the decoration would urge me to go forward and do a great deal more for him and for England, as the army thought only of him and loved both. My interview then ended."

Early in April, having recovered from his second wound, he returned to France. The last letter received from him was to his sister. It is dated the 18th of May :—

"On the 14th we remained in pouring rain in trenches, bitterly cold, and then reached the camp at 3 a.m. very tired, and my feet a little frost-bitten. On the 15th and 16th we rested, and are moving back again. I am writing to you from a trench. We are up to our knees in mud, and it has rained since yesterday when we came here, but we are all hale and hearty. My boots and puttees are soaked, but must remain so for three more nights. I never felt fitter, though tired of this sort of warfare. I hope I never get shelled again like the other day. It is a very high trial sitting still and enormous shells bursting, blowing all the ground up, able to do nothing, and just waiting for your turn."

His turn came the day after this letter was received. On the 28th of May I received a letter from Lord Charles Beresford, who had just arrived from France. He announced the death of Francis, shot through the heart, dying in a quarter of an hour. He had come over with an officer who had attended his burial. It was better to have got the news in a sympathetic letter from an old friend, rather than a curt telegram from the War Office.

By his last letter to me, after the fifteen hours' bombardment on the 13th, when the Ninth stuck it out, I gathered that whatever happened he would never retire, but meant to do or die. He had great charm, good looks, strength and purpose in important things ; was utterly careless in the conventionalities of life, too much being crowded into the same day ; but in greater questions he had a strong will, great determination, and would not be denied. No loss was more genuinely felt than Francis's and Rivy's death.

I received a large number of letters and telegrams.

"ROYAL PAVILION, ALDERSHOT.

"To FIELD-MARSHAL LORD GRENFELL,
  "OVERSTONE PARK, NORTHAMPTON.

"The Queen and I are grieved beyond words that your gallant nephew has fallen in battle. I was proud to give him his nobly-earned Victoria Cross, and trusted he might live to wear it for many years. Our heartfelt sympathy with you.
"GEORGE R.I."

"May 1915.

"Deeply grieved by sad news. Please accept and convey to his sisters my heartfelt sympathy in your great sorrow.
"ALFONSO R."

"G.H.Q.   May 28th.

"To FIELD-MARSHAL LORD GRENFELL,
  "OVERSTONE PARK, NORTHAMPTON.

"Will you let me condole with you on the loss of your gallant and distinguished nephew in the 9th Lancers after having been twice wounded. His record of gallantry is unsurpassed.
"FIELD-MARSHAL SIR JOHN FRENCH."

From COLONEL HON. C. WILLOUGHBY, 9th Lancers.

"Francis joined the Ninth just about the time I got command when we were stationed at Rawal Pindi. I was very pleased to get him as a subaltern. He was one of the hardest working officers I ever knew, always doing his best whether at work or play, thereby setting a high example to others. His good horsemanship and quick eye soon made him a very valuable cavalry officer ; this combination also brought him to the fore in the polo world, where he did such good work for the regiment in after years. The Ninth have lost a good officer, a high-principled gentleman, and a real good sportsman.

"As you probably know, Francis was a dear friend of ours ; I was very, very fond of him."

From COLONEL DESMOND BEALE-BROWNE.

"Francis has left a memory and example that will never fail. A braver soul never stepped. His high ideals, and boundless enthusiasm for the regiment and the cause in which we are fighting, was an example we shall never forget, and the regiment is indeed proud to think that it had Francis Grenfell in its ranks. I only so regret he did not live to hear the praise bestowed on the regiment which he loved so dearly, and whose honour he had done so much to maintain."

From MAJOR-GENERAL VESEY DAWSON.

"I must send you a line of sympathy in your great sorrow. I know how much you will feel the loss of your two nephews, and I do indeed feel for you. I feel that the loss is really the country's, for we do not produce too many gallant, brilliant soldiers such as the one who is just gone. He would, I think, have gone far in the profession if he had lived, and it seems indeed sad that he should have been taken."

From Major-General Hon. John Lindley.

* * * * * * *

"He was a right gallant soul, and the very embodiment of all the manly virtues that go to make a cavalry leader, and the cavalry have sustained a loss well-nigh irreparable. Modest, bold, and as cool as a cucumber, it will be many a day before the men of his squadron and the 9th Lancers get another leader like him.

"Well, he has gone to join his twin soul, and a more gallant pair never entered this world together."

From Lieut.-Colonel Edgar Brassey.

"I feel I must write to you to express my deepest sympathy in the sad news about poor Francis. Whatever else this war may bring about, the absence of the Twins can never fail to be noticed and lamented. I have known them for over twenty years, have played cricket with them, hunted with them, and played polo with them; and for myself, I can say that there is nobody, even in the long list of friends who have gone in this last nine months, who will be missed more than Francis and Rivy. We may be sure that neither would have wished to be separated or to die a more glorious death, and the example of the Grenfell family, not forgetting poor Robert, who was also a friend of mine, will stand for ever in the annals of the British army."

From Mr. Charles Murray of Loch Carron.

"I must send one word to say with what sorrow I read of dear Francis's death. He is almost the last of Alasdair's close friends who has remained to us, and he always kept up his friendship. Only the other day he came in to cheer me up when I was ill in London, and, as with Rivy, it is a great break with the past. I ever hoped that Francis and Rivy would live to distinguish themselves, and that Francis, a keen and good soldier, would follow in your footsteps and some day lead British forces in the field. It could not be, and, with others of the best, the boys have gone from us, and I know how deeply you will feel the blow."

From WALDORF ASTOR.

"The deaths of Francis and Rivy mean an irreplaceable loss to their friends, and bring grief to all who knew them intimately. We are all forced to bear trouble, anxiety, and bereavement, but apart from this there is perhaps the greatest tragedy in the real loss inflicted on the country. Never will two persons like them be found.

"Kipling asks in a poem, 'Who dies if England lives?' One feels inclined to say, 'How can England live as one has known her if such as these die one after the other?'

"None of the blows caused by the war have been so hard, and have even by comparison tended to diminish this one, or to lessen the grief I and many others feel."

From the DUKE OF TECK (MARQUESS OF CAMBRIDGE).

"I have just heard the sad news about the death of poor Francis. I am so deeply sorry for you in the loss of your other nephew. What a blank the death of the 'Grenfell Twins' will cause to a good many people, my wife and I amongst them; but to you it means much more, and I ask you to accept my deep and heartfelt sympathy in your great sorrow."

From SIR HEREWARD WAKE, King's Royal Rifles

"I am so grieved about Francis. I would like to send you a word of sympathy. Francis compelled the love of every one who knew him, and there are hundreds of people who will mourn his death. I think there never was a more gallant pair of soldiers or Englishmen than those two."

From Dr. MILLER MAGUIRE.

"I esteem it an honour to testify to the great merits of your brave nephews, Francis and Rivy Grenfell. I had intimate knowledge of their zeal for their noble profession, and all connected with its study, almost to the date of their death. They excelled in cavalry exercises and in the ardent devotion to that particular branch.

"Francis was making himself well versed in European and American campaigns, and no doubt would have been placed high in any Staff College tests had he been spared; but almost from the desk of study

'He rushed into the field, and, foremost fighting, fell.'"

It was on April 14, 1915, that I said good-bye to Francis. He walked home with me round Portman Square, after dining with his sister. He was cheerful at the idea of rejoining his squadron, but no doubt the knowledge that Rivy would not be with him was in his mind. He spoke with enthusiasm of his squadron and regiment, and the chances of war, and was very hopeful as to the future. He was happy in the belief that the most distinguished regiment in the army was the 9th Lancers, and that he commanded the best squadron in the best regiment of the best fighting army in the world. He mentioned that he had refused a Staff appointment after being twice wounded, being so greatly impressed by the unanimous response which was made for his call for volunteers to save the guns at Audregnies. This touched him deeply, and he said that no offer of Staff service would ever induce him to leave his squadron.

We said good-bye, and I think both felt that we should not meet again. Of that, personally, I had a strong presentiment.

The Twins, so happy in their generation, are now together ; freed from the feverish anxieties they suffered ere they went to war, they are linked in a new and better life, surely for them one full of activity and high service.

" Time takes them home that we loved, fair names and famous,
 To the soft long sleep, to the broad sweet bosom of death ;
 But the flower of their souls he shall not take away to shame
  us,
 Nor the lips lack song for ever that now lack breath.
 For with us shall the music and perfume that die not dwell,
 Though the dead to our dead bid welcome, and we farewell."

FRANCIS AND
RIVERSDALE GRENFELL

CHAPTER I.

1880–1899.

ONCE when Rivy had had a bad smash at
polo he spent some time in hospital. " It
seems odd to say so," he wrote to Francis, " but
I enjoyed it immensely. What lucky people we
are, taking an interest in so many things ! This
was another side that I had not yet seen." I set
down these words at the beginning of this short
record, for they sum up the attitude of the two
brothers to life. Few people can have had a larger
share of the happiness of youth, for not only had
they ample opportunity of action and experience,
but they bore within themselves the secret of
joy. They never ceased to wonder at the mag-
nificence of the world, and they carried a divine
innocence into soldiering and travel and sport
and business, and not least into the shadows of

the Great War. In the comfortable age before
1914 they were among the best known and most
popular young men of their day, and some picture
of their doings may be of interest as a memorial
of a vanished world. The coming of war upon
their eager life is a type of the experience of
all their countrymen, and a revelation of the
inner quality of that land which has so often
puzzled herself and her neighbours. But I write
especially, as the friend of Francis and Rivy,
for their many friends : who, before memory
dies, may wish some record of two of the most
endearing and generous spirits that ever " before
their time into the dust went down."

I.

Francis Octavius Grenfell and Riversdale
Nonus Grenfell were born at Hatchlands, Guild-
ford, on September 4, 1880, the twin sons of
Pascoe Du Pre Grenfell and Sofia Grenfell his
wife. Family history would be out of place in
such a narrative as this, and I do not propose
to discuss the intricate question of the Grenfell
pedigree, and whether kin can be counted with
the great figures of Sir Richard Grenville of the
Revenge, or Sir Bevil, the Cavalier, of Lansdown
Heath. It is sufficient to say that they came of

an old Cornish strain, which in their case was double-distilled, for their parents were cousins. A Grenfell fought at Waterloo and lost a leg ; their mother's father, Admiral John Grenfell of the Brazilian Navy, was Lord Cochrane's second in command, and performed many famous exploits, notably the cutting out and destruction of the Spanish flagship *Esmeralda*, in the midst of an armed squadron. His brother, Sydney, was a British admiral, distinguished in the China War. Their father's brother is Field-Marshal Lord Grenfell. Of their own brothers, Pascoe served and died in the Matabele War ; Robert fell gloriously in the charge of the 21st Lancers at Omdurman ; Harold did brilliantly as a column commander in South Africa ; and Arthur won the D.S.O. at the Battle of the Somme. A cousin, Claude Grenfell, was killed at Spion Kop ; and all the world knows of their other cousins, Lord Desborough's sons, who will live because of Julian's poetry and their mother's exquisite memoir in the literature as well as in the history of England. There are many famous fighting stocks among our people, but there can be few with a more stirring record than this.

A word should be said of their uncle, their mother's brother, because he was a hero of romance to the boys in their youth, and they loved to dwell upon his amazing doings. Francis and Rivy were always gentle in their ways, and for this very reason they had a weakness for a stout swashbuckler. Admiral Sir Harry Grenfell was a British sailor after the eighteenth-century pattern. His gallantry was proverbial in the navy of his day, and he had various medals for saving life at sea. There must have been much of Julian's spirit in him, for he had an insatiable zest for adventure and fighting, and when he could not get it in the way of duty he went out to look for it. Among other things he was middle-weight champion of the navy. There is a story of him with which Rivy once delighted an American public dinner. He went ashore with some brother officers at Constantinople, and drifted to a music hall, where he found an immense Turk offering fifty dollars to any one in the audience who could knock him out in five rounds. Harry Grenfell promptly accepted the challenge. He put on the gloves wrongly, and stood awkwardly, so that the challenger thought him a novice and gave him some easy openings. Taking advantage of one of them, he stretched his antagonist on the floor. On recovering his senses, the Turk advanced to the footlights and announced in the pure accents of Limehouse, "Gen'l'men, the hexibition is closed." Then, going over to Grenfell's corner, he shook him warmly by the hand, whispering, " You're no bloody lamb." There is another tale which may be apocryphal, but which the Twins cherished as an example of how their uncle looked at things. Once Admiral Grenfell was dispatched in his ship to some Pacific isle to arrest and bring to Sydney a chief who had eaten a missionary. The chief was duly arrested, but during the long voyage back the British admiral came to entertain the highest respect for his qualities as a man. The upshot was that he dumped him down on some desert island and returned to report to his superiors that, having gone most carefully into the case, he had come to the conclusion that the missionary had been entirely in the wrong.

II.

The first seven years of their life were spent at Hatchlands. As the youngest members of a large family they were a perpetual delight to their sisters, and their brothers vied with each other in directing their small feet in the paths of sport. They were solemn, self-possessed children, quiet in their ways, and as inseparable as the two sides of a coin. They would lurk peacefully for hours in corners, and once a short-sighted visitor sat down on them on a drawing-room sofa and nearly smothered them. As babies they were not so much alike, but as they grew older they became perfect doubles, puzzling everybody, including their mother, who often gave the wrong one medicine. At Hatchlands they acquired two red fox-terriers, known as the Gingers, who were as much alike as their masters. Only the Twins knew the Gingers apart, and only the Gingers could tell which twin was which. They had an air of serious cheerfulness, especially in their misdeeds, which was so endearing that it disarmed wrath ; and they played their confusing twinship for all it was worth. Once, when they had been quarrelling—for, in the immortal phrase of the *Irish R.M.*, they " fought bitter and regular, like man and wife " —their mother caught up one (she did not know which), set him on her knee, and scolded him heartily. When she stopped, the culprit said in a calm, meditative voice, " You certainly do look very jolly when you are angry, 'cos your eyes shine so." They were very unpunctual, and had always convincing excuses. " Why are you late this time ? " their father once asked despairingly. " Well, it's all the fault of the housemaid," was the answer. " She's so selfish. She won't lend me her stud, and mine has gone down a rabbit-hole " One of their traits was a genius

THE TWINS AT THE AGE OF EIGHT.

for getting hold of the wrong word. They used to give sixpence to the Christmas " waits," till their father reduced the bounty because of the growing number of the applicants. " Only pennies this year," the Twins announced to the waiting mob, " 'cos there's a chrysalis in the City." This habit long remained to them. At school they invited their parents to come down and see the new chapel " disinfected " by the Bishop.

Having seven brothers adepts at every form of sport, Francis and Rivy were early " entered " to most games. They played a kind of polo, mounted on walking-sticks, at the age of four. They soon learned to ride, and when hounds met anywhere in the neighbourhood they invariably contrived to be run away with by their ponies, and avoided lessons for that day. Their first pony was a communal possession with the name of Kitty, an aged family pet, which they took charge of and groomed themselves. Presently Kitty grew so infirm that she had to disappear from the world. They were told that Kitty had gone to stay with her mother, and complained that it was cool of her to go off without consulting them. A little later the coachman, in a moment of forgetfulness, presented them with one of Kitty's hoofs. Said one twin to an-

other in bewilderment, " What an extraordinary
mother poor Kitty must have ! " At that time
they took a very solemn and matter-of-fact view
of life. At their first pantomime they saw a
rustic ballet of beautiful " farm workers," and
for some time afterwards perplexed the occupants
of every farm they visited by asking where the
pretty girls lived. At their second pantomime
they were with their uncle in the stage-box, and
argued so vigorously with the clown that he
climbed up beside them, to their mingled joy
and embarrassment. Their engaging gravity had
no self-consciousness ; they talked to their elders
as they talked to each other. A relation who
pronounced certain words in a bygone fashion,
once at breakfast busied himself at the sideboard.
" Who says tea and who says corfee ? " he asked.
The serious voice of Rivy replied, " Personally
I always say *coffee*, but I'm too small to have
any."

In 1887 the family moved to Wilton Park,
near Beaconsfield, where their father had spent
most of his childhood. It had belonged to Mr.
George Du Pre, his uncle, who for nearly forty
years had been M.P. for Bucks and a colleague
of Disraeli. There the Twins were in clover,
and could indulge to the full their love of games
and passion for animals. In the park they raced

their ponies and hunted rabbits with the Gingers; they acquired several ferrets, and the favourite home of the ferret bag was the best armchair in the drawing-room. The worst poacher in the village was their habitual ally, and became so much attached to them and the family that he had to be made under-keeper. They had a cricket ground where they practised assiduously, and were bowled to by the sons and grandsons of the boys who had bowled to their father. They organized boys' matches, arranging everything themselves. Their mother once asked them to let her know what they wanted for tea after the match. "Don't trouble, mother," was the answer. "We have ordered two hundred buns."

III.

In 1887 they went to Mr. Edgar's school at Temple Grove, East Sheen, where their seven brothers had been before them. At that time they were bent on learning every game, but had no ambition to excel in lessons. They both played cricket and football for the school, and occasionally brought home a prize, the wrong twin being invariably congratulated on the achievement. In their schooldays their spelling was original and ingenious. To one who was

about to become their brother-in-law they wrote :
" I can gratcherlate you, she is a niece girl."
Apropos of a wet day they achieved this memo-
rable sentence : " It pordanpord." The word
deserves admission to the weather vocabulary
of the English tongue.

In 1894 they went to Eton, where their grand-
father, father, six brothers, and many cousins
had been before them. They began in Mr.
Arthur Benson's house, but next year went to
that of Mr. Walter Durnford, who was one of
the chief family friends. Their name was sufficient passport in that home of long traditions,
for three of their brothers had played in the
Eleven, and they rapidly became very popular
and dominant figures in the school. In 1898
Francis was Master of the Beagles, and Rivy
Whip. At the time the pack was most indif-
ferently housed, so the Twins raised a fund to
build, on the piece of land known as Agar's
Plough, the kennels which are now in use. They
wrote letters—generally wrongly addressed—to a
multitude of old Etonians, including the late Lord
Salisbury, and received subscriptions and letters
—notably one from Lord Rosebery—which they
cherished as heirlooms. " The Head Mastei,"
Mr. Durnford writes, " was never safe from
having his majestic progress through the playing

fields arrested by one of the Twins conveying some petition concerned with the great project, and the Bursar—not renowned for his acceptance of new ideas—capitulated before the unceasing attack." In 1899 Francis was in the Eleven, and in the match against Harrow at Lord's, at a critical point in the game, he and Mr. H. K. Longman, of Mr. Radcliffe's house, made 170 runs for no wickets. That year he established a bold innovation. Formerly the two Elevens kept apart at lunch ; Francis, though it was his first appearance in the historic match, decreed that they should sit together, and ever since this excellent practice has been followed.

At Eton they showed little interest in books, and later were wont to lament to each other that they had left school wholly uneducated. But they learned other things—the gift of leadership, for instance, and the power of getting alongside all varieties of human nature. They discovered, too, an uncommon knack of obtaining what they wanted by their gentle persistence and radiant charm of manner. They had a way of taking things for granted, and giving large orders which were generally fulfilled. Being desirous to have flowers on their small window-sill, they wrote to the gardener at Wilton to send them some " rowderdendrons." It appeared afterwards that they meant geraniums, but an under-gardener was discovered faithfully digging up an enormous bush, which would have filled their little room, let alone the window. They always worked in couples, and used their similarity in looks shamelessly for various unconstitutional purposes. During the winter one would answer for both, so that the other could get off to hunt. Once the trick was badly given away by the huntsman appearing at supper with blood trickling down his sleeve. Taken unawares, he explained that he had had a fall on a heap of stones. Hunting had now become a passion with both, and during one exeat they settled to go to Melton, hired horses to meet them at a very early train, and ordered a hansom to be at the door at 6 a.m. The cab never appeared, and they missed the train. They managed to get half-way to the meet in a slow train, and then *took a special* and had a first-class day. Coming back in the evening they told Frankie Rhodes the trouble they had had, and he insisted on paying for the special.

Both of them had an astonishing gift of getting on friendly terms with every sort of dignitary. The complete simplicity and candour of the two slim, dark boys was not to be resisted. There is a legend, probably untrue, that Francis once begged a sovereign from the Head to tip a hunt-servant, and got it ! Another tale can be vouched for. After one of the many consultations about the new kennels, Dr. Warre walked down the street with his arm in Francis's. He stopped to speak to some one, and at the same moment Francis met a friend, upon which the Head overheard the following conversation. Said the friend, " Fancy you walking arm-in-arm with the Head ! Why, he terrifies me ! " Said Francis, " I don't see why the poor man shouldn't have pals among us. It's bad enough to be Head, without having to go without pals." And here is an adventure of Rivy's. He was asked by Miss Bulteel, who was then in waiting on Princess Beatrice, to tea at Windsor Castle. He marched in, and ascended the first staircase he saw. There he found a kind old lady, who asked him whom he wanted to see, and on Rivy's explaining told him he had come in by the wrong entrance. She summoned a liveried giant, and bade him show the way to Miss Bulteel's room. The giant bowed low to Rivy and walked backward before him along several passages and up and down staircases. Finally the crab-like progress halted before a door, and with another low bow Rivy was asked what name. When he gave it the giant drew himself up, flushed and said, " Oh, is that all ? You can go in." Afterwards Rivy found out that he had wandered up the Queen's private staircase, that the old lady was the Empress-Dowager of Germany, and that the footman had taken him for a foreign royalty. This was not the last of Rivy's odd experiences in court circles.

Mr. Walter Durnford has been so kind as to set down his recollections of the Twins.

"I have been asked to contribute to the memoir of Francis and Riversdale Grenfell something bearing on their life as boys at Eton. It is not a very easy task, for though their memory is still fresh and strong in the mind of the writer, life at school, with its regularity, its ordered course of work and play, does not present, as a rule, startling features or occasions which lend themselves to description. Month succeeds month, and year follows year, with such quiet regularity that almost before one realizes the change the small boy has grown into the big boy, and the big boy is preparing to take his place in the great world.

"The 'Twins'—for so we always called them, and it is indeed impossible to dissociate them in our memory—came to Eton in 1894, and a year later entered my house, where their brothers Harold, Arthur, and Robert had preceded them— a funny little pair, so like one another that they were the despair of masters who only saw them occasionally; and even their tutor, who saw them perpetually, never really knew them apart till the last year they were at Eton. Francis, writing to him after Rivy's death, says: 'Rivy used to like you best, I think, when some one gave him a yellow ticket and you used, when you came round, to pretend to be furious and curse me instead of him.'

"Like most brothers, they fought. In the same letter Francis writes: 'You, who used with difficulty to part us after fighting in old days, know what we were to each other'; and, indeed, they had at bottom that love for each other which,

THE TWINS WITH THE ETON BEAGLES.

it seems to me, only twin brothers have ; nor do I believe that they were ever happy if for many hours they were separated.

" To say that they were diligent would be absurd. They vexed the souls of masters in whose forms they found them-selves, and on whom they sometimes played off their wonderful likeness with diabolical ingenuity ; they vexed the soul of their tutor, who had to see that, somehow or other, they scraped through their tale of work. But it was impossible to be angry with them for long, for their invincible cheerfulness blunted the wrath of justly indignant teachers ; and all the time they were learning, unconsciously perhaps, but still learning, the lessons which were to make them so greatly beloved in after life—lessons of kindness, of thoughtfulness, of perseverance, of straight and honourable conduct—the fruit of which will be seen in the later pages of this book. So the years slipped by—happy years for both of them—until they found themselves in that position which is perhaps the most delightful that the English boy can attain to—' swells,' with troops of admiring friends, and a recognized position as people of mark in the school. Such a position is not free from danger, and boys' heads are easily turned by it ; but the Twins never lost the simplicity which was one of their most engaging characteristics, and they retained, as all boys do not, the heart of a boy to the end of their schooldays."

Mr. Durnford notes how little they changed during their school life. It is the testimony of all their friends at all their stages. They possessed a certain childlikeness, the ardour and innocence and unworldliness of the dawn of life, the charm of which was never rubbed off by experience. The one change during the Eton years was that Rivy began unconsciously to charge himself with Francis's future. A list of their school friends—

even of their intimate friends—would be so large as to be meaningless, but I fancy, looking back, that their closest friendships were with Waldorf Astor, Lord Esmé Gordon-Lennox, Lord Francis Scott, and Paul Phipps. From a letter of the last-named I quote a sentence: "Even in those days Rivy had begun to adopt the protecting, almost paternal, interest in Francis's career which he preserved all his life. In the summer in which Francis got into the Eleven it was Rivy who took out his twin and sternly made him practise fielding, just as in later life he would conscientiously read some book which he had heard recommended, not for his own instruction or amusement, but in order that he might pass it on, if found suitable, to Francis."

IV.

The summer of 1899 was their last term at Eton. The time was coming very near when their paths must diverge. Their father had died in 1896, and they lost their mother in 1898. Wilton Park had been given up some time before, and the family was scattering, their many brothers being already settled in various professions. Their uncle, Lord Grenfell, was their guardian, and few guardians can ever have fulfilled more devotedly and successfully their trust, as this narrative will bear witness. I quote from a letter written by him in September 1898 from Cairo :—

"MY DEAR TWINS,—By the death of your mother I become your guardian, and shall have to settle with Cecil as to your future careers. . . . You may rely upon me to do all I can to help you. But you are getting on now, and soon you will have to depend on your own energy for your success in life. You will not be rich, and you will have to work for your living, as your father and I have had to do before you. Though you have both been good boys, and have all the feelings of gentlemen, and have never caused your father or mother any anxiety, you have neither of you (as far as I can learn) taken any great interest in your studies. You must remember that in your future life you will not be able to do nothing but amuse yourselves, and I do trust that for this next year, whether you remain at Eton or not, you will work hard and try to learn all you can to improve your minds and fit yourselves for the future.

"I always received so much kindness from your father and mother when I was young, that you may depend on my helping you as much as I can ; and when I am in England my house will always produce a corner for you and a bottle of the best. You have your brothers also to advise and help you. But to be successful in life you must depend on your own exertions, and therefore I hope you will work hard and learn to be punctual and support your masters.

"Read your Bibles, and shoot well ahead of the cock pheasants ; and if you are ever in any difficulty that your brothers can't help you in, come to your very affectionate

"UNCLE FRANCIS."

"P.S.—Since writing this, I have heard of dear Robert's death.* He died a gallant death for his Queen and country. . . . Well ! he is with God—and your mother—and there we can afford to leave him."

---

* At the Battle of Omdurman.

Both would fain have followed the main Grenfell tradition and become soldiers, but their means forbade. One of them must choose a more lucrative calling, and the duty fell to Rivy, as having entered the world a few minutes later than his Twin. In any case he would have given first choice to Francis, to whom he had come to regard himself as *in loco parentis*. In this assignment Francis was the luckier, for he was born for the army. Indeed, both were, for it is hard to believe that Rivy had any aptitude for high finance, and he had beyond doubt the makings of a fine soldier. There was a very real difference between their minds : for Rivy, as we shall see, discovered later a restless interest in politics and a good deal of ambition for that career, while Francis never wavered in his devotion to his profession ; but the aptitudes of both might well have been satisfied by the multifarious requirements of modern soldiering.

When they left Eton the Twins seemed exact replicas in tastes and interests, and they were as like as two peas in person. That summer Francis went to Inverness to join the Seaforth Militia, with a view to a commission later in the 60th. He stayed at Loch Carron with his friend Alasdair Murray, who a few months later was to fall with the Grenadier Guards in South Africa. While he

was out stalking one day, Rivy arrived, was shown
to his room, and changed into a suit of Francis's
country clothes. When he rang the bell a footman appeared, who looked once at him and fled.
" Something terrible has happened to Mr. Grenfell on the hill," he told his fellows in the servants'
hall. " His ghost is sitting in his room ! "

Francis caught typhoid that autumn in Inverness, and for several months was seriously ill.
In December 1899 he was sent off to the Cape for
a sea voyage, and so began those wanderings
which were to fill the rest of his life. Meantime
Rivy had become a decorous clerk in the Bank of
England. The Twins had left boyhood behind
them.

CHAPTER II.

1900–1904.

To pass from the proud position of a leader at school or college to the blank insignificance of the outer world is a trying experience for most people, but the Twins were not conscious of any difficulty. They were too utterly unsentimental to moon over the past; they had always been very modest about themselves and their accomplishments, and they were profoundly excited about the new life which lay before them. Rivy was soon absorbed in the City (after making a fruitless attempt to enlist when war broke out), learning a strange jargon, puzzling over unfamiliar standards of value, and beginning to lament a defective education. Francis had a harder fate. Typhoid checked him on the threshold of soldiering, and he had the unpleasant duty of spending a year in trying to get well.

He sailed for South Africa in December 1899, for the sake of the voyage, intending to return by the next boat. At the Cape, however, he fell in with his brother John, who was acting as war correspondent, and was fired with the wish to see another brother, Harold, who was then in command of Brabant's Horse. During the voyage out he had suffered much from what he thought was lumbago, but which was really an affection of the spine due to the fever, and his time in South Africa was one long bout of pain. He went by sea to East London, and then up country to join Harold. He trekked for some days in a springless wagon, which did his back no good, and finally collapsed in a Dutch farm eighteen miles from Cradock, and had to finish his journey lying in a chair on a cart. After some days in Cape Town he went to the baths at Caledon, where his health improved ; but the return voyage in March 1900 knocked him out again, and he came home worse than when he had started.

But an English summer and a Scots autumn cured him. The Duke and Duchess of Somerset took him yachting with them in the Hebrides, and those windy seas restored him to health. One of the party was the Gaekwar of Baroda, of whom Francis reported : " I have made pals with the Maharajah, and am going to dine with him in London, and he is going to show me all his jewels and Indian costumes. I believe his pearls are like eggs. He asked me to stay with him in India—he has got over 300 horses, very good tiger-shooting and pig-sticking. He said, ' Your visit won't be official, so you need bring no suite.' He pronounced it like ' suit,' so I said, ' All right, only my old blue one.' " Lady Anne Murray allowed him to camp at Loch Carron, where he killed his first stag and his first salmon. Here is his record of two days, in a letter to Miss Sybil Murray : " I left Loch Carron yesterday ; beastly day—pouring and blowing. However, I fished hard at Balgey, got bored and soaked, and at 4—just as Donald said it was hopeless—whack ! a salmon. In the end we got five trout and one salmon. This morning I got up at 6.30, went on the hill, and after a good stalk got up to four beasts. One rose, then another, and flukily and luckily I got both—one a fair beast, the other a good one. By this time it was 12.30. I ran home to Loch Carron, ordered a cart, had a glass of the best port, and set out in torrents of rain for Balgey. Met Donald, who said I was luny. Fished in a fearful storm, and at 6.30, very dark, misty, and wet, whack ! a salmon. Up at 6.30, two stags ; four miles' run home, fourteen miles' drive, salmon ; three miles on here—not a bad day ! If that is not sport, what is ? Did you ever hear such luck as two salmon in two days to a novice ? "

In October he was back in London, where he was passed fit by a medical board, and ordered to Cairo to join the militia battalion of the Seaforth Highlanders. He had himself measured for a kilt, which, as he says, made him very shy. After some hunting with Rivy at Melton, and various shooting parties—at one of which he was shot in the leg by a neighbouring gun on two successive days !—he sailed in November for Egypt.

There he spent the better part of four months, working for his army examination, playing a good deal of polo, and occasionally riding steeple-chases. He found the life boring, for he was eager to get into regimental work, and Egypt, while the war was going on in South Africa, was too much of a backwater for a soldier. Lord Cromer greatly impressed him, and he saw a good deal of him as a friend of Windham Baring's. " To hear him talk is worth hearing," he wrote to Rivy, " as he is quite the biggest man we have —in fact, in his place, bigger than Chamberlain. He has told me not to chuck polo, and that work five hours a day is ample." He got his commission in the 60th in May 1901, when he was at Malta, whither he had gone in the end of March. There he acted as an extra A.D.C. to his uncle, Lord Grenfell, who was then Governor, and laboured to cope with the intricacies of Maltese etiquette. On one occasion the Archbishop of Malta attended a large reception at the Palace, and his devout flock wished to kiss his hand as soon as he appeared in the doorway. Francis attempted to move him on, and was haughtily told, " You do not know who I am. I am the Archbishop." The extra A.D.C., knowing only one brand of archbishop, sought another member of the Staff in despair, saying, " The door is quite blocked, because that old gentleman has gone luny and thinks himself the Archbishop of Canterbury." At Malta Rivy joined him for a little, and the Twins rode many races on their uncle's ponies. There used to be an irritating bell rung in a chapel close to the Palace, and one day to the joy of the household it suddenly stopped. Lord Grenfell, anxious to discover the reason, found that the Twins had driven the bell-ringer from his post by pelting him with coal !

On their way home it is recorded that in Paris, in some café or other public place, they forgathered with a French soldier. In their zeal for information they asked him in their best Ollendorff, " Qu'est-ce que vous pensez de l'affaire Dreyfus ? " The question, delivered in a clear, boyish voice at a moment when French feeling on the matter was hectic, secured an embarrassing attention for the travellers.

The Twins with Lord Grenfell at Malta, April 1901.

In the autumn of 1901 Francis was with the 60th at Cork, whence he sailed in December for South Africa. He indited a farewell letter to Rivy, " the final time I will write you about my affairs before we meet again, you a wealthy City man, and I a poor subaltern with a V.C." There are some characteristic messages. " Send me cuttings out of papers sometimes, such as very good speeches, debates or leading articles in the *Times* [he had always a craze for leading articles]. You might send me a few big races and some hunts, also any of our pals' weddings, big cricket matches, or any divorce of some pal of ours, or anything startling in the papers. . . . Work hard at the City, keep fit, teetotal, and mind the girls " [his sisters]. A month later he was planted on a hilltop near Harrismith.

The last months of the South African War were not an enlivening moment to start on the profession of arms. The great hours of the campaign were over, and the war had become a thing of barbed wire and blockhouses, varied by more or less futile " drives " when the Boer commandos evaded the snares ingeniously set in their sight. Francis would have been very happy in the " drives," and did his best to get his old friend Harry Rawlinson * to take him

* Now General Lord Rawlinson.

with him; but the discipline of the army confined him to garrison work, and, instead of being with the hunt, he had to content himself with the duties of earth-stopper. His letters chiefly tell of meetings with other bored friends, such as Francis Scott, in casual blockhouses, and of the amassing of live stock. "I have no right to any horses; however, I have two good riding ones, including a polo pony, and three cart ponies." . . . . "I have bought a Cape cart of a Dutchman, newly done up, for £10. I really gave him £10 as a tip, and he went and stole the Cape cart." . . . . "I have now got four ponies, two good ones. Rather an odd thing happened about one of the ponies we commandeered. First time I used him was to send him to get some milk. Funnily enough, it seemed he belonged to the milkman." He started polo under difficulties, and complained that no shooting was possible at Harrismith, as "all the buck lay the same way as the Boers." He discovered that he had been meant by Providence for cavalry rather than infantry—a discovery hastened by the arrival of the 14th Hussars. "By Jove," he writes, "there is a difference between cavalry and infantry. I mess with them. At mess the sergeant-major says, 'What will you drink, sir? I have only whisky, lime-juice, and champagne.'" It is difficult to see how this re-

sourcefulness in drinks can have mattered much
to Francis, who, like Rivy, was a consistent teetotaller ; but he liked a lordly way of doing
things. "The only way I can make you feel
what this life is," he wrote, "is to compare it
to your being asked to stay at Melton for five
or six months, being offered mounts every day,
hearing of the best of sport, and seeing every
one going out and not being allowed by your
taskmaster to go. That describes this job exactly ; only with hunting, you know, you can
hunt next year or a year to come, but here I know
I shall never get another job of Boer pursuing."
He deeply sympathized with the view of an Eton
friend who turned up one day with the words,
"O Lord! Twin, which is the way to England?
I'll not be a soldier a week after I get home!"

The tedium of those Harrismith days was not
improved by Rivy's letters—for from now onward
the Twins maintained a methodical correspondence. Rivy was enjoying that golden time which
comes only once in life—a popular young man's
first entrance into the great world. He was by
way of learning the ropes in the City, and engaged
in small but complex transactions on Francis's
account, since he had the management of the
latter's slender patrimony. The letters are full
of City gossip, which greatly perplexed the lone

soldier at Harrismith. " Love to all, including
the Jew man who helped to make £27 for me.
Southern Pacifics sound good, and are in the
papers. I can't find Leopoldinas anywhere under
City, Stock Exchange, or Markets. What does
Yankees mean ? Yankee what ? I can't find that
either."

In January 1902, Rivy was given a post in the
office of the Charter Trust, of which his brother
Arthur was a director and Lord Grey chairman.
But he had plenty of time to spare for amuse-
ments, and his letters were full of tantalizing
accounts of runs with the Quorn and the Belvoir
and the Windsor drag, dances, week-ends at
Cliveden, Ascot, and Westonbirt, parties in London, endless bachelor dinners. Rivy was always
an excellent letter writer, and at this stage had
not the acute educational interest which appeared later, though I find him advising Francis
to learn the *Times* leaders by heart to improve
his style, " because they are very good English."
Usually his epistles are vivid diaries of his doings.
The record of old runs is apt to be " like mouldy
wedding cake," but here is a description of a
day with Waldorf Astor's drag.

" I rode Jim Mackenzie's runaway ; they put an india-
rubber bit in his mouth which was useless. We started over
the rails at Hall Barn, and then went right-handed up the

hill to the farm at the top. Near the farm my quad took charge, so I sat back and rode at one of those large white gates, hit it very hard, pecked very badly, and was shot off. I was soon up. We then checked in Slough road. We started off again down that ride where I once fell over a hurdle with the drag. The grey * ran away and took full charge ; first down a steep hill over some rails ; then across the road into a plough, where I got a little pull ; then over about four fences, and then in jumping a small one he landed on his head and lay there for about five minutes. I took the saddle off and let him get his wind ; then I hacked to the check, which was at the Gerrard's Cross gate of Wilton Park. We started again up the park over the stile in the corner, then right-handed over those two wire fences between the farm and Pitland ; then bore a little to the left—you know where I mean—through the fence between the larches and that steep lane. I remembered there was a pit somewhere there, but couldn't remember where. To my horror I found myself unable to stop about five yards from it. So I sat like a mouse, and the brute slithered half-way down, then jumped about ten feet, and away again, as it was open at the bottom. Dalmeny thought I was dead, when to his surprise he looked down and saw me half-way across the next field."

Rivy's letters contain lists of the friends he ran across, the ladies he danced with, and occasional gobbets of political news like this : " Rosebery wrote to the *Times* yesterday to cut off all relations with C.-Bannerman ; which has made rather an excitement." Or bibliographic notes such as : " I will send you out next mail a very good book, *Science and Education*, by Professor

* It turned out afterwards that this grey had at some time or other had its jaw broken on both sides, with the result that it got the bit against the jaw bone and could not feel it.

Huxley, which I have marked in several places—
a sort of book you can read over again. I have
often noticed lately, in the leading articles in the
Times, 'as Professor Huxley says.'" Printing-
house Square has rarely had a more faithful
adherent. But here is a record of a startling
adventure.

"I got a wire from Horace Farquhar [Lord Farquhar]
asking me to go and dance at 10.30, so I dined at home and
went round. On taking off my coat I asked if there were
many people. 'Yes, my lord—the King and Queen.' I
walked upstairs where a lot of people were standing, and I
ought to have stayed there. But like an ass I barged into
the drawing-room, where every one was standing at attention.
The King walked up and shook me warmly by the hand. I
didn't know whether to kiss it or kneel down or what, so I
just calmly said, 'How do you do, sir?' At that he started
off in the most fluent French. 'What, sir?' More fluent
French. 'I beg your pardon, sir?' I didn't understand one
word he said, so he repeated the French, in which I caught the
words 'tante' and 'malade.' 'I beg your pardon, sir?' I
said, standing on one leg. Then he said in English, 'And how
is your aunt?' 'Very well indeed, sir.' 'Oh no, the one who
has been so ill. I am so glad she is much better.' 'Thank
you, sir, she is very well.' I simply didn't know what to
do or say. 'Are you going to stay here long?' (I thought
he meant stay dancing.) 'No, sir; I am going away early.'
'I hope you will stay here some time, as you are such a great
traveller. How do you propose to go home?' (He meant
home to France.) 'I thought of going by the Underground,
sir.' That put an end to it. I gave a sort of bow, and went
over and shook hands with Lady Farquhar. I then sneaked
into the corridor, where we stood about for some time. Afterwards I saw Horace Farquhar, and he said the King had

taken me for a Frenchman called Paul de Jaucourt, nephew of Mrs. Hartmann, who has had bronchitis. Princess Pless heard my conversation with the King, so I asked her if I had made a blazing fool of myself. She said I had got out of it very well, and never noticed anything except she could not make out why he spoke French. After I had gone out he asked, 'Who was that?' 'Grenfell!' 'Good gracious, I have been talking French to him and asking about his aunt! Why didn't they tell me?' He was rather sick, I believe, as he hates making mistakes. . . . Everybody has heard the story, and roars with laughter."

In March Francis was allowed to join his brother Harold's column in the Western Transvaal, and for the next three months had all the movement he wanted. It was just after Lord Methuen's *contretemps*, and the Boer general opposed to them was the redoubtable Delarey. He found himself among old friends, such as Jack Stuart-Wortley and Freddy Guest, and the details of the life approximated to the cavalry standard. "Old H. is splendid. Catch him roughing it! He has got an A1 tent he bought at home with every sort of thing inside. We halt, and in about five minutes it looks as if we had been there for ever. . . . On trek his bridles, buckles, boots, breeches, etc., look as if he was at Melton hunting, they are so clean. I have got three niggers now, and hope to be the same." On 1st April they just missed rounding up a Boer convoy, and Francis was speedily disillusioned as to what galloping meant in that kind of war. " Your opinion is—and mine used to be—that you saw Boers and galloped at the charge, same speed as the Derby ; but it is very different. Here you have a horse with a kettle hung on him, coat, mackintosh, water bottle, cap, man, 200 rounds ammunition, and into the bargain a great crock. You can imagine the pace we go." He was pessimistic, too, about the war and its progress. " How they can say we have conquered this country Heaven knows. If you leave your blockhouse you get sniped, and if you go out with 500 men you get jolly well kicked back into camp. The Boer roams about the whole country as he likes, and yet it is ours." On the 11th, however, he obtained his desire, and was for the first time in a serious action at Moedwil, where his column had six killed and fifty-three wounded. " Up to now I had no time to notice wounded, or even to feel in a funk. But the moment the show stopped I felt as if I had had a good shaking and hated it." He was mentioned in dispatches, to his intense annoyance. " Let those that deserve it be mentioned. My job was only a sort of head-waiter's."

On the 6th of June peace was signed. Harold started for home, and Francis found himself in Johannesburg. There, as the army broke up, he met a host of friends, and sampled also the local society. He played polo, raced, sold horses, speculated a little like every junior officer at the time, and was lucky enough, through good advice, to make in diamond mines a considerable sum of money, which enabled him to think seriously of going into the cavalry. Spurred on by Rivy's entreaties, he did his best to learn something about gold-mining, and became terribly confused in his earnest study of the markets. He gives amusing pictures of the queer, cosmopolitan life of the place—amusing because they are the work of a shrewd and yet most ingenuous observer. Every one who remembers those days on the Rand will appreciate such a note as this: "Old B. has made a lot of money here. The other day he found in the card-room a Jew learning poker. He gave £10 for another Jew's seat, and then took £300 off the learning Jew. He wasn't born yesterday."

Presently he returned to his regiment at Harrismith, and stayed with it till the end of the year. He had outstayed his leave on the Rand, and when he arrived at Harrismith was put under arrest. The man who preceded him in his interview with the commanding officer was overcome by the heat, and was carried out in a dead faint. When Francis was led into the presence he observed cheerfully to the colonel, " I hope, sir, you are not going to be so hard on me as you've been on that poor chap." *Risu solvitur curia*.

Sir Hereward Wake, who was with him during those months, writes : " I played with Francis, Geoffrey Shakerley, and Roddy Brownlow in what was, I think, the first polo tournament Francis played in. It was at Harrismith. There were thirteen teams in, and we (*i.e.* the 60th) won. We used to have the most awful rags in the mess in those days, and I will never forget Francis. He was by far the worst of us, though he was a teetotaller." He made strenuous efforts to get away from South Africa, and an A.D.C.-ship to Lord Dudley in Ireland and the chance of service in Somaliland were discussed in turn in the brothers' letters. But nothing happened till the battalion was ordered to India, and Francis returned to England in February 1903.

At this period Rivy's letters are the better reading. New horizons were opening up for him everywhere, and he gave Francis the benefit of his enlightenment. That summer and winter, in the intervals of dancing, polo, and hunting, he reflected profoundly, and his own and Francis's careers were the object of his thoughts. He had discovered that he was very badly educated, and was determined to remedy the defect. " It don't matter a damn, I do believe, not having learned at Eton as long as one does so now." So he set to work at a queer assortment of books, and sent the results of his cogitations to Francis. Here are some extracts :—

"Any one can improve his memory. The best way is learning by heart, no matter what, and then, when you think you know it, say it or write it. After two or three days you are sure to forget it again, and then, instead of looking at the book, *strain your mind* and try to remember it. Above all things, always keep your mind employed. One great man (I forget which) used to see a number on a door, say 69, and try to remember what had happened in all the years ending in 69. Or see a horse, and try to recall how many you have seen that day. When riding or walking, try to recollect the sayings or events in the last book you have read, or the daily paper. Asquith always learns things by heart. He never wastes a minute ; as soon as he has nothing to do he picks up some book. He reads till 1.30 every night ; when driving to the Temple next morning he thinks over what he has read. Result : he has a marvellous memory, and knows everything."

"I am reading Rose's *Napoleon*, and will send it to you. What a wonder he was ! Never spent a moment of his life without learning something. . . . I went and saw the Coronation from Montagu House. The usual show, but I had a good yarn with Francis Scott."

"I enclose a copy of an essay from Bacon's book. Learn it by heart if you can. I have, and think it a clinker."

"Since 1st June I've read Macaulay's essays on Chatham, Clive, and Warren Hastings. Then an excellent book, *Map of Life*, by Lecky ; Bacon's *Essays ; Life of Napoleon*, by

Rose, and *Last Phase,* by Rosebery. I have also finished *Life of Macaulay,* most interesting. I've always wondered how our great politicians and literary chaps lived. . . . I also send you a Shakespeare. I learned Antony's harangue to the Romans after Cæsar's death by heart. I am also trying to learn a little about electricity and railroad organization, so have my time filled up. I tried to buy Moltke's *Life,* but it is 25s. ! *Pickwick Papers* I also send you. I have always avoided these sort of books, but Dickens's works are miles funnier than the rotten novels one now sees. We shall have to start a correspondence comparing the books we read. Probably you will hate the ones I like, and *vice versa,* but I'm sure you will love Clive."

" I have learned one thing by my reading and conversation with professors. You and I go at a subject all wrong. Don't read *Life of Wellington* and the history of his wars, but take a period and study it as a whole."

There are pages of explanation of City matters, which Francis cannot have read unmoved, as Rivy during the summer contrived by injudicious investment to lose a considerable sum of money for him. It is curious to find Rivy with his ambitions herding among the *rastaquouère* crowd of minor speculators, intent on little gambles in matters where he had no serious knowledge. Sometimes the wave made by some big vessel carried forward his small cockle-shell, but more often it submerged it, and there was a sad explanatory letter to his partner at Harrismith.

About this time—when such explanations were over—Rivy took to lecturing Francis on his duties,

and tried to inspire him with his own aims.
" H. writes to Arthur that you have the wildest
ideas—want to return at once, get into a cavalry
regiment and play polo—and that the sooner you
chuck polo and look at the serious side of life
the better. I am awfully disappointed, as I
hoped to plug at the City and get to the top of
the tree, and you at the top of soldiering, instead
of a loafer who only plays polo. England would
have finished the war sooner if we had had more
Kitcheners and fewer polo pros." That was all
very well, but in nearly every letter of Rivy's
there were lyrical accounts of his own games at
Ranelagh and Roehampton, and a good deal
more about horse-coping and bachelor dinners
than about books. Francis, in his Harrismith
solitude, may well have considered that his phy-
sician himself needed a little healing. And when
at Christmas the same earnest apostle of self-
culture went to Paris on education intent, the
exile in South Africa may have reflected that he
too would be ready to follow a path of duty
which led through dinners at the Embassy, *Les
Folies Dramatiques*, Maxim's, and the Café de
Paris.

One pleasant trait of Rivy's was that he felt
bound to pass on to Francis any good talk he
heard, and faithfully to describe his week-ends.

He was at Terling when the news came of the signature of peace in South Africa.

"Lord Rayleigh is a very scientific fellow; in fact, he is about a generation in front of his time. I don't think I have ever enjoyed a Sunday so much. Lady Rayleigh is Arthur Balfour's sister. The party included Arthur Balfour, Lord and Lady Ribblesdale, Lord and Lady Cobham, Miss Lyttelton, Lord and Lady Cranborne, and Mr. Haldane, K.C., who is supposed to be the cleverest lawyer and philosopher. It was ripping to hear those fellows talk.

"On Saturday Balfour got a cable from Kitchener to say the voting was going very close, which sent me to bed with rather a headache. However, they kept the telegraph office open all night, and at ten o'clock Sunday morning he got a telegram to say, 'Delegates have signed peace; Secretary for War is consulting Prime Minister about publishing news.' In the afternoon he got another telegram to say that they would publish the news at four o'clock. I was rather in hopes that they would keep it till Parliament met on Monday, and then one would have got it about five hours in front of everybody else. After dinner on Saturday they discussed peace. Balfour said he did not like the telegram at all, but what made him hopeful was that the City was so confident. In all probability the City knew more about it than he did, as he only heard the news from Kitchener and Milner, against telegrams from all over Africa. This came as rather an eye-opener to me when one considered that fellows in the City were looking to Arthur Balfour as knowing about ten thousand times more than they did. . . .

"I had a good talk to Haldane late in the evening about America, the Shipping Combine, etc. He said that the great difference between the American and the Englishman was that the American boy was always thinking how soon he could get on in business, while the latter was always thinking how long he could keep out of it. . . .

"Ribblesdale is the best fellow you ever met. For five

minutes he talks about Shakespeare, and for ten minutes about fox-hunting."

It was on this visit that Rivy heard Mr. Balfour and Lord Rayleigh praising *Alice in Wonderland*. Deeply impressed, he bought the book as soon as he returned to London and read it earnestly. To his horror he saw no sense in it. Then it struck him that it might be meant as nonsense, and he had another try, when he concluded that it was rather funny. But he remained disappointed. He had hoped for something that would afford political enlightenment.

In February 1903 Francis came home, under orders for India. I think it was on this occasion that Rivy met him at Southampton and found that he had omitted to bring any money. Francis, having spent all his during the voyage, was in the same position. Both happened to be wearing suits of an identical brown. Stewards and other people expecting tips, pursuing Francis, were suddenly and awfully faced by the apparent duplication of their quarry. They gave up the quest and retired to reflect on their sins.

The brothers were together for the better part of seven months, so their faithful correspondence ceased. They lived with their sister Dolores at 17 Hans Row, and had a pleasant summer of balls and polo-playing. Their likeness was a great amusement to them, and often at dances they would change partners, who were quite unconscious of the difference. Rivy used to breakfast at eight and leave for the City, while Francis got up at a more leisurely hour, to the confusion of a new parlourmaid. "This is a funny place," she declared. "One of the gentlemen has had two breakfasts, and the other has disappeared without having any."

In September Rivy departed for America " to learn business," taking with him a case of his brother's champagne as provender for the road. He visited many cities, both in the United States and in Canada, acquired a mass of miscellaneous information, and made the acquaintance of Mr. Bonbright, in whose London house he afterwards became a partner. The diary which he kept on his tour showed that he would have made a good commercial journalist, for he had the liveliest interest in all new business organizations and mechanical processes, and considerable power of describing them. He met a variety of people, from Mr. Chauncey Depew and Mr. Hill, the railway magnate, to some of the American polo players whom he was afterwards to know better. The trip was an admirable bit of education, for it gave him a host of new friends, and the weeks of solid work which he put in in a Trust office in

New York were an excellent apprenticeship. The diary is as serious as the works of Mr. Samuel Smiles, but now and then he deals with other things than business. In Denver he went to church.

" As I was approaching it a nice-looking man accosted me. ' Guess we're late. My name is James; what's yours ? ' ' Grenfell,' says I, wondering what he wanted with me. As we entered the church my new friend told me I might sit in his pew. I never enjoyed a service so much. It was high church. They had women in the choir and cheery hymns. Just before the sermon the Rector, instead of announcing banns of marriage as I expected, said, ' Friends, Christmas is nearing. I'm going to have a rare old Christmas. These last three years I've been starving myself, but I'm going to alter all that. Everybody, I hope, will join in making Christmas happy. Why, in old times they used to carry the parson out on a stretcher.' I thought this the most outspoken, first-class parson I had yet struck."

To his delight he found Waldorf Astor in New York, and the two returned home together in December.

Meantime Francis had left for India, and early in November was with the 60th at Rawal Pindi. There his soul was at once torn with longings. The sight of racing studs and much polo inflamed his ambition, and the proximity of the 9th Lancers awoke all his hankerings for the cavalry. He had wanted to join the 17th Lancers, but now transferred his affections to the

Ninth, which contained many old friends. At first he did his best to be patient, aided by a wise letter from Harry Rawlinson and some trenchant remarks from Rivy. But the longing could not be repressed, and the *cri de cœur* breaks out in every letter. " I dined with the 9th last week. By Jove, Mate, a cavalry regiment is different . . . ten old Etonians . . . nicest chaps on earth . . . Colonel won the National . . . a fizzer," and so on. His chief argument was his great keenness on polo, about which he could rouse little enthusiasm in his own regiment. He argued thence to military superiority. " David Campbell * is adjutant, and fairly puts in ginger. You can imagine a show run by David Campbell, who is very good at polo, mad keen soldier, won the Grand National and Grand Military." In December it was : " By Jove, Mate, I do hate this walking. It does make one's mouth water to see those chaps riding." He did not much approve either of the way the foot-slogging manœuvres were con- ducted. " The one idea of the umpire is to see who has the most men. If you have a battalion very strongly entrenched and are fought by one and a half battalions, you are said to be beaten. Yet in South Africa fifty Boers delayed and made

* Major-General Sir David Campbell, who commanded the 21st Division in the Great War.

it dashed uncomfortable for Buller's whole army."
He finished off with the novel plea : " Infantry
soldiering is dashed rot and dashed *expensive*.
I have worn out all my walking boots, and now
my calf has grown so I cannot get on my polo
boots ! " In despair he besought Rivy to see if
the *Daily Telegraph* would send him as correspondent with the Tibet Expedition.

So the first part of 1904 was passed by Francis
in a state of considerable disgruntlement. Not
that he was unhappy. He had fallen in love with
India and the modest pleasures of a soldier's
life there ; but the vision of the joys of cavalry
was always at hand to tantalize him. The 9th
Lancers warmly urged him to transfer, and he
wanted it done at once, that he might have the
summer for polo practice and then, as he said,
" win everything next year." But the War Office
does not move in such torrential fashion, and, more-
over, his uncle and his relations generally were
doubtful of the wisdom of the step ; so for months
there was a complicated correspondence in which
Francis filled the part of the moth desiring a
star. He did his best to work for his examination
in Hindustani, a language which he reprobated
on the ground that it was without " literature
and fairy tales." But he very often broke loose,
and went off to polo matches and steeplechases

up and down India, excusing himself to the censorious Rivy thus : " While working I thought to myself, ' Why make life a burden, and chuck everything, and then probably fail ? By not buying ponies now I cannot get a chance for next year.' So I got leave and started off——" The result appeared in the next letter. " Yesterday I rode in a steeplechase. Arrived on the course full of dash and no end of a swell. Left it like the chap who last fought Pedlar Palmer—black eye, stupid, hand like an apple, and lame ! " Then he would return penitently to his books. " The munshi says I haven't a chance of passing. By Jove, Mate, I am beginning to feel the effects of never learning Latin Prose at Eton."

About this time the correspondence between the brothers was remarkably candid. Rivy had a typist to dictate to, Francis scribed with his own (usually damaged) hand ; so when Rivy's epistles were scrappy Francis had something to say. " I have a tremendous lot to tell you, but I am so angry with your letter this mail that I won't write more. It is too bad, Mate. I sweat like blazes to write to you, and I receive a typewritten letter from you signed by an infernal clerk." Each gives advice to the other with the utmost frankness. For example, Francis : " Take a tip from me, old boy : go gingerly with the reforms in your office. Don't rush in and say, 'This is dashed badly done. In America it is done like this.' We are all so apt to do this, as our family is enthusiastic and impatient. It only gets chaps' backs up and makes everything more awkward." And Rivy : " You say the races are awful rot. Why the deuce do you attend them then ? Oughtn't you to be spending your time much better ? If you spent the time with a book in your hand instead of at some silly race meeting, where you loaf the whole day, it would do you more good." And again on the cavalry question : " I would like to see all your ponies break down and draw your nose to the millstone [*sic*]. At this moment you look on the Ninth as everything. In a few years you will probably be looking on them as the greatest rotters. Remember that the majority of men who have become great have done so through the necessity of having to work to get their bread and butter." But Francis occasionally got back on his mentor. " Yours of 29th February to hand—rather a rotter. It does seem funny you starting polo again. Here am I in the home of polo—a ground half a mile off—and I haven't played at all, and don't seem to want to. Your letter saying I was so out in £ S. D. made me put up all my ponies for sale." Francis had considerably outrun the constable in his expenditure, and Rivy had taken him gravely to task, adding morosely that things were so bad in the City that stockbrokers were beginning to pick up cigarette ends in the street.

His wrestlings with Hindustani had soured Francis on the intellectual life, towards which Rivy sought to goad him. His letters contain some sensible remarks on the Tariff Reform controversy then raging, but that is all, save for the flickering interest in art revealed by one postscript : " What is the name of the chap who did the pictures of naked ladies at Hertford House, and those things in the Duchess's room at Blenheim ? Not Boucher, was it ? " Rivy, on the other hand, was grappling manfully with his education. In January he was reading Creevey, and much struck by his resemblance to Sir Henry Campbell-Bannerman. " It shows that the times of Pitt, which I have always looked on as beyond reproach, differed very little from our own." At Terling he met Raymond Asquith—" whom I have always heard of as the cleverest person of the day "—and was much impressed by Raymond's habits. " When I arrived at the Rayleighs' there were a whole lot of fellows talking in the smoke-room and blinking at the fire, except one. Of course you can guess who it was—Asquith reading in a corner. In the train coming up, while I read

four pages of my book he read twenty of his."
He was desperately afraid of getting the reputation of a *flâneur*. " Harry Longman said to me
quite seriously, ' I congratulate you, Rivy.' ' What
for ? ' says I. ' I hear you and Francis are millionaires.' . . . What a curse it is the way our
family, especially you and I, seem to get talked
about ! Serious people look on people who are
always talked about with suspicion. I hate being
a sort of Jubilee Juggins of the gossip world."

He procured a coach, with whom he read
history several hours in the week, and he strove
to move in intellectual society. " I had a topping
evening. I had written to ask two professor
chaps to dinner, one of them von Halle, head
professor in Berlin, the other Mackinder. You
would have laughed if you had seen them. They
came and dined at the Bath Club at 8.15. About
7.30 I got into such a funk at what the devil I
should say to them that I got Cecil to come as
well. However, as always happens with that
sort of chap, they were most easy to talk to and
most entertaining." He attended political meetings, notably Mr. Chamberlain's in the City ;
he dined with Lord Rosebery the evening before
the opening of Parliament, and he treasured
every fragment of good talk he heard to send to
Francis. At Easter he went again to Paris, and

wrote an amusing account of a stag hunt at Fontainebleau.   What with one thing and another he had a most varied spring and summer, and his diary is filled with polo matches, City gossip, and the record of dinner-table conversation in about equal proportions.   Here are some specimens of the last :—

"Met Jack Morgan,* who told me this anecdote.   His mother went to see an ostrich farm in California.   The keeper, pointing to two fine ostriches, said, ' Those are Lord and Lady Bobs.   Bobs is a very docile animal, and very nice to Lady Bobs.   Those two are Mr. and Mrs. Morgan.   Old Morgan is a crusty brute, and will have nothing to say to his wife.' "

"Met Harry Rawlinson in the Park. . Talked of Stonewall Jackson, his power as a leader of men and judge of character. Lee was the thinker and Jackson the actor.   Harry R. poked my pony in the ribs and said, ' What sort of thing is that ? ' whereat my beast promptly landed his a kick in the stomach."

"After dinner went to an ' At Home ' of Mrs. Sidney Webb. Met some rum-looking coves there.   Had a talk with Mrs. Webb about fiscal policy.   A Free Trader joined in, and I argued disgracefully, proved nothing, expressed myself badly, and was rather trodden on by the Free Trader, who knew his points."

"Dined with Lady Salisbury in Arlington Street—a jolly party, composed of Lord Hugh Cecil, Winston Churchill, Lady Mabel Palmer, Neil Primrose, Lady Crewe, Lady Aldra Acheson, and Sir Edgar Vincent.   Sat next and bucked to Lady Aldra.   W. Churchill held forth at dinner to the whole

---

* Mr. Pierpont Morgan, the younger.

table, discussing invasion. Salisbury said he thought that
if one was going to make a speech one ought to do nothing
else the whole day."

"Dined with Lord Rosebery. Party included Dowager
Duchess of Manchester, Revelstoke, Crewe, Lady Sibyl Grant,
Dalmeny, Mr. and Lady E. Guinness, Brodrick, Haldane,
Lady Gerard, etc. After dinner Lord Rosebery and Brodrick
chaffed each other. Rosebery quoted some speech of Gladstone's. ' Yes,' says Brodrick, ' but he continued to say '—
and quoted some more of the same speech. How on earth
do these chaps get their memories ? . . . Rosebery came and
talked to me. I do look up to that man. . . . He told a
story of Lord Robert Cecil, who is noted, like all Cecils, for
his ignorance of horses. A case came up in the courts at
which reference was made to a horse's knees. ' Which knee—
fore or hind ? ' asks Cecil."

During that summer Rivy had a somewhat
serious love affair. He was not what is commonly
called susceptible, and made ready friendships
with women as he made them with men. His
letters are full of the " jolly little ladies " and
" capital girls " that he was always meeting.
But now he stumbled on something rather like a
" grand passion," and he sighed in vain. The
experience made him for the rest of his life curiously tender and sympathetic towards others in a
like case. I never heard Rivy laugh at even the
crudest romance. For a little he was very miserable, and in the orthodox way he thought of
travel. There was another reason why he should

go abroad. The South African market was in a bad state, and since his work on the Charter Trust was concerned with South Africa, he thought it right that he should go out there and judge things for himself. At the back of his head was a plan to join Francis in India. Sir Clinton Dawkins encouraged the project, so on 23rd July he sailed for the Cape.

Meantime in India the unwilling rifleman was hovering about the candle of the 9th Lancers. He applied for a transfer, and then, on the advice of his relations, withdrew his application. He was much encouraged by a letter from Sir Douglas Haig, who was then Inspector-General of Cavalry in India.

"DEAR FRANCIS GRENFELL,—I shall be delighted to assist you in any way I can. First, I think you wise to join the Cavalry, because you will have greater opportunities of acting on your own, and more independence than in the Infantry.

"Next, as to the regiment. You can't do better than join the 9th.

"Lastly, as to working it. Don't fret about two or three years' seniority. You must risk something, especially in the Cavalry. Officers seem to play leap-frog over one another in the most surprising manner nowadays. So my advice is to take the first chance you can of joining the 9th, either by transfer or exchange. . . . Arrange to come and stay with me here for two or three weeks, and we will do our best to push the matter through."

For the rest Francis's letters are filled mainly

with obscure details about a buggy to be bought
at home, notes about matches and race meetings,
and boisterous complaints about the aridness of
Rivy's epistles. " A very moderate letter from you.
. . . You say nothing of the National, nothing
of Cecil, Harold, Arthur, the girls or the uncle.
Buck up, old boy, and make that typewriter
move. Are you so busy you can only spare
time to write ' Yours, Rivy ' (badly written), and
even have to hand the envelope to be addressed
by a chap whose writing made me think it was a
bill ? " To which Rivy retorts : " The last two
pages of your letter are occupied with telling me
of a pony of yours that was gelded. Cannot you
find something more interesting and instructive
than this to tell me ? I don't care a blow whether
every pony in India is gelded to-morrow morning."
But the gelding, judging by his exploits, was
worthy of a letter. Says Francis later : " My
pony Snipe that was gelded has recovered wonderfully, and laid out two syces. One he kicked in
the kidneys. The next day he boxed the new
syce, got free, and caught him on the eye with
his hind-leg ; so he also lies for dead."

In spite of his anxieties about his future,
Francis had a pleasant year. He played in polo
teams which won the championships at Poona
and Umballa, and at the latter place he met

Lord Kitchener, who, to his surprise, knew all about his cavalry ambitions and approved them. The news that Rivy was to visit him stirred him to immense exertions, for he was determined that the traveller should have the best that India could offer. He was now genuinely in love with the country.

" It is the best I've struck, once you've forgotten England. It is not that it is so much cheaper (which it is), but the great thing I find is that every one is so much poorer. No bachelor seems to have more than about £600 a year, and many £100, and the married about £2,000. I am looked on as a Hoggenheimer, whereas in England you contrast with fellows like Harold Brassey. I live like a king—servants, carts, horses galore. What more can one want except a wife—but on that point there's a famine in the land."

CHAPTER III.

1904–1905.

I AM inclined to take the autumn of 1904 as the end of the first clearly marked stage in the Twins' lives after leaving Eton. It was a transition period in which both were trying to decide what they wanted. Francis had not yet found the military groove best suited to him, but he now knew what it was, and he was on the eve of acquiring a true scientific interest in his profession. Rivy, having played about in the City for several years, had acquired a good deal of miscellaneous knowledge, which fell far short, unfortunately, of a rigorous business training. But he had learned one thing— the value of education—and he was very busy making up leeway. Indeed, he was educating himself apparently rather for Parliament than for business, for all his models were orators and statesmen. Both, too, after experimenting in many sports, had reached the conclusion that polo was the game for them, and were laboriously studying to excel.

Francis in India was wildly excited at the news of Rivy's visit, and sketched the most far-reaching programme. The whole sporting and educational wealth of Hindustan must be at his brother's disposal. Rivy hoped to arrive before Christmas and stay several months, and this was Francis's scheme :—

" Go to Calcutta. Stay with Curzon as Viceroy's guest. Deuce of a dog! Just like going to England and staying with the King. In mornings see Calcutta trade. Afternoon, racing; see hundreds of pals. Get a little pig-sticking (too early). Then go to Cawnpore—biggest trade centre in India. Then do Agra, Delhi, and on to Pindi ; see F. G. ; on to Peshawur and Khyber Pass. Across to Quetta and see other end of frontier. Back, play a little polo, perhaps Sialkote tournament. Go to Lucknow; play in open tournament in Civil Service Cup race week. Pig stick; arrange tiger shoot. If possible (doubtful), you have time to go to Mysore for an elephant. This tiger-shooting and pig-sticking will take you into March. Come to Patiala. If I play for 9th I shall be there practising for Inter-Regimental. Come to Meerut Inter-Regimental week. End of March, compete in Kadir Cup—pig-sticking, best sport in the world. If you only let me know in time, can buy you three good horses. Train to Bombay ; arrange to see trade and town. Tip F. G., get on steamer, and leave about 1st April, having had best time in the world."

This delirious programme was not to be fulfilled. Rivy travelled through Natal and the Transvaal, disliked Johannesburg, visited his brother John's copper mine at Messina, north of Pietersburg, and finally reached Rhodesia, where he had a little shooting and began to enjoy himself. " Its crab is that it is full of English gentlemen instead of Jew boys ; consequently everything is run very much *à la amateur* instead of professional." But on 24th November he sat down in Buluwayo to write Francis a melancholy letter, which is worth quoting for the light it casts on Rivy's mind.

" I have to write a very sad letter to tell you that I cannot come to India after all. The cursed City seems to have turned round, and a small boom to be in progress. The result is that the Charter Trust want me home. . . . I have thoroughly thought the position over the last five days, and, greatly against my will, decided to return.

" These are the arguments :—

" In favour of staying my full time in Rhodesia and then going to India :

" (1.) I am comfortably off, and at present don't want more money. I am far more anxious to be a clever and common-sense man with sufficient money than an ordinary rich ' City man ' ; and so it is far better for me to travel and see the world and return to England in four months, which, after all, is not much time to lose, when one has the remainder of one's life to spend in business.

" (2.) It is far easier when you are away from home to stay away, than it is when you are at home to get leave to go away.

" (3.) I went straight into the City from Eton, with the intention of travelling when I was twenty-three or twenty-four.

" (4.) I urgently want to see you and talk with you, Mate.

" (5.) You have taken enormous trouble and expense on

my behalf, and bought ponies, and I have bought a dashed rifle for £60 from John which I don't want.

" (6.) Clinton Dawkins has sent me letters which I suppose would help me to go anywhere.

"Arguments in favour of curtailing my stay here and abandoning India:

" (1.) I have worked hard for five years in the City with the idea of making business my career; and to miss ' good times ' when you have been through the ' bad times ' and learned fairly thoroughly your trade is the same thing as a soldier studying soldiering during a long peace and then not going to the war when the chance comes.

" (2.) The idea of my travelling in America and Africa has been, besides getting a good education, to learn the opportunities that offer in the countries, to turn them to some good. I have already lost a good chance by Americans having done well (and especially the railways I saw) since I have been in Africa.

" (3.) It has been dashed good of the Charter Trust to let me go away two years running (though without a salary) and see the world.

" (4.) In India I should be enjoying myself, and should learn nothing of business.

" (5.) There is a possibility of John and Arthur floating a Copper Co. within the next six months. Having learned all about the copper, I should look an uncommon fool if it was brought out and everybody made money except you and me, who were playing polo in India.

"With these opinions, I think it is my duty to chuck my pleasure and great desire and return at once to business. O my God, Mate, I am sick about it though, and fear you will be greatly disappointed."

So by the end of the year Rivy was back in London, full of large schemes of reading. In South Africa he had ploughed his way through

Lecky's *History*, and Morley's *Burke* had whetted his interest in that great writer. So as soon as he got home he purchased Burke in twelve volumes, and Butler's *Sermons*, this latter on the ground that it was a book " that Chatham, Pitt, and Gladstone studied." He was very grateful for any advice which gave him a clue to help him through the labyrinth of his education. " Hugh Cecil told some one that every day of his life he reads a good speech and tries to reason out all the original ideas which must have brought the thoughts into the speaker's mind, and studies how they begin and end their speeches." Lord Hugh was now by way of becoming his exemplar in many things—" an absolute clinker and brilliant in every way ; he makes one roar with laughter, quotes Shakespeare, etc., and makes most clever jokes."

In January 1905 he stayed at Hatfield, and wrote to Francis a long account of his visit. The Lyttons, Lady Mabel Palmer (Countess Grey), Miss Maud Lyttelton (Mrs. Hugh Wyndham), the Harry Whites, Lady Edward Cecil, Lord Hugh, and George Peel were there.

" After dinner acted charades. They chose most difficult words—in fact, names of people that my education had never reached—yet Hugh Cecil guessed every one. . . . They have a most magnificent library, and a chapel bang in the centre of the house ; indeed, to go from one end of the house to the

other you have to pass through the chapel, only the altar
being consecrated. . . . In a quarter of an hour one learns
history by simply walking through these rooms. . . . It
seems to me that people like the Cecils simply cannot help
being clever ; in each room are pictures of Prime Ministers,
etc. Four of their ancestors have been Prime Ministers ! . . .
They fairly do teach their children. The Salisbury boy, aged
eleven, has read nearly all the family papers. They have a
little boy three years old, and I assure you he knows far
more English poetry than me.''

Francis, too, was not without his taste of
society. He went to Calcutta for the Viceroy's
Cup, saw the races from the Cooch Behar box,
and dined with Lord Kitchener. " Bachelor dinner," he wrote, " and played pool afterwards. Met
Hood,* who is in command of a battleship here.
He's a proper good chap. Didn't care a damn
for Lord K. ; bellowed at him as if he was Jones.
Such a change after frightened soldiers."

Rivy's devotion to duty was to be rewarded.
On his return to the City he found that he could
be spared for a couple of months, and on 3rd
February he was in the Dover train on his way
to India, " studying Burke on American Taxa-
tion."

Rivy's Indian trip was one of the most successful expeditions that ever fell to a young man's

---

* Rear-Admiral Hon. H. L. A. Hood, who went down in the
Invincible at the Battle of Jutland.

lot. Nothing happened to mar its perfection, and he returned in three months, having had his fill of every form of Indian sport, and having won the blue ribbon of a game which he had never tried before. He picked up Waldorf Astor at Brindisi, and the two of them were deathly sea-sick on the voyage to Port Said. " Went to dinner, found the captain and one other out of forty passengers, ate three courses, and was sick between each," is an entry in his diary. He arrived at Bombay on 17th February, and on the 19th found Francis at Bareilly. Francis had grown a moustache, which just made the Twins distinguishable.

For the next month Rivy was the intelligent tourist bent on seeing as many of the sights as were consistent with polo, pig-sticking, and the persevering study of Burke. He went first to Agra ; then to Meerut, where he played a good deal of polo and had his first experience of pig-sticking, riding Francis's horse " Barmaid "; then to Umballa to stay with Eustace Crawley ; then to Patiala, where the Settlement Commissioner, Major Young, instructed him in Indian problems, and he had a little pig-sticking; then to Peshawur by way of Umballa and Lahore. He was back in Lucknow by 17th March, staying with Henry Guest, and then on to Benares. At Bareilly he went to a "pig-sticking week" with Francis, Henry Guest, and Lord Charles Fitzmaurice, and had four days of it. His diary records his disappointment: "Most of us came to the conclusion that even if the pig were there it could not be compared to fox-hunting. One wants to find pig every fifteen minutes to make it really amusing. Another drawback to my mind is that when a party goes out, if one part enjoys it the other members have probably had no rides, and so been bored to death. Charlie Fitzmaurice was very fed up." After that he returned to Agra to see the Pearl Mosque again, and then to Delhi, where he studied the battlefield of the Ridge. On 26th March he and Francis started for the ground of the Kadir Cup meeting, which that year was held in the Sherpur country.

The Kadir Cup is the Derby of the sport of pig-sticking, and is run off each spring in a selected area of jungle. Rivy had been first introduced to that noble game exactly twenty-three days previously, so his boldness in competing may be likened to that of a man who takes on the mastership of a famous pack of hounds after a few weeks in the hunting field, or a novice who leaves the jumps of a riding school to ride in the Grand National. I quote the tale of his exploit exactly as he wrote it in his diary. The field was enormous, there being over a hundred competitors.

" *26th March, Sunday.*
" Got to camp about 12.30. Most delightful situation. Generals Mahon * and Douglas Haig there, and we made many pals. At 5 p.m. F. G. and I went out riding and schooled the horses, nearly slaying two wretched cattle in the attempt. Found a sow and galloped after her. A jolly evening, and to bed early.

" *27th March, Monday.*
" Breakfast at 6.45. The first round of the Kadir was run off. I drew General Mahon and Douglas Haig, and rode ' Cocos ' first. We were in the third heat, and got away after being one hour on the line. I was first on to the pig, being some way in front ; but my horse slipped up on the flat, and so General Haig got the spear. Francis made all the running in his heat, and won. We then rode on an elephant and watched the remaining heats.

" F. G. was beaten on position in his second heat by Barrett. He was first on the pig, and did most of the riding ; but it jinked, and Barrett got the spear. I was on the line for nearly three hours in my second heat. We had three false starts, and lost our pig in some very heavy goul after a short ride. At last we got away, with every one shouting at different pig from the elephants. Haig (again drawing the same heat) and I got on to a very fast sow, and had a heavy gallop ; and I speared her, only to find we had gone after the wrong one, and the heat was declared off !

" *28th March, Tuesday.*
" The line started at 8. Our heat was first run off. We were slipped up to an old pig, and I, getting up to him first, soon speared. Two hours after I had to run off the next round, in rather a hot heat of Last and Kennard. We got a good start to a fast pig. ' Barmaid ' went like a gun, and

---

* General Mahon had won the Kadir Cup in 1888.

soon got a long lead, and I got first spear.   F. G. drew White
and Learmouth.   He rode 'Recluse' and cut out most of the
work; but the pig jinked right back, and let in White, who
got the spear.

"29*th March, Wednesday.*

"A red-letter day for me.   The line started at 8.30 for the
semi-finals.   Three heats were left in—two threes and a four.
I was in the four heat, composed of Barrett (15th Hussars), Last,
Neilson (4th Hussars), and myself.   We were quite two and a
half hours on the line, and had three false starts.   At last we
got away to a jinking pig.   Last and I did most of the riding,
with Barrett some way behind.   Last nearly got a spear once,
and we bumped unavoidably.   The pig then jinked right
back to Barrett, who was about to spear him, when I came up
with a rush.   The pig jinked across my front; he speared him
very lightly behind, while I ran him through and broke my
spear.   The umpire said he would give it to Barrett if he
could show blood, but luckily for me he couldn't.   It would
have been bad luck for me if I had lost this spear, as I did
most of the riding.   So I qualified for the final.   'Barmaid'
went wonderfully, but got rather beat, as it was a severe heat.

"On returning to the line I was met by F. G. and General
Mahon.   F. G. then became stud groom.   We took 'Barmaid'
and let her stand in the river, and then she had three good
rolls in the sand.   After an hour's rest we started for the
final—Pritchard (2nd Lancers) (on 'Toffee,' the horse which
F. G. tried to get me for £100, but Pritchard would only sell
'Barmaid' for £40), Ritchie of the 15th, and myself.   We
soon got a good start on a pig, and I was on him first and
drew some way to the front, and just got a spear as he jumped
into a nullah.   The mare jumped right over him and knocked
the spear, which was smashed, out of my hand.   The pig
carried my spear some yards.   It was a grand feeling as the
spear ran into him to think I'd won the Kadir.   Pritchard
naturally appealed, as I'd dropped the spear, but the committee upheld the umpire's decision.

"In the afternoon the Hog-hunter's Cup, a point-to-point

THE TWINS AFTER THE KADIR CUP.

over three and a half miles, was run, and F. G. won easily on
'Cocos,' going a line of his own the whole way. This rather
made people stare, our carrying off the two chief events of
the day. F. G. and I then went out and found the pig killed
in the final which had been lost, and hacked thirteen miles to
Gujraula and caught the train for Calcutta. . . . I went
round to the Viceregal Lodge, and found Nipper Poynter as
A.D.C. there. I shall never forget the look of astonishment
on his face when I told him I'd won the Kadir."

So much for the interloping Rivy's performance in a " game he did not understand." The
history of the Kadir Cup, and indeed of Indian
sport, hardly contains a parallel. It was the
first time that the Cup had left India. He spent
the next few weeks shooting at Cooch Behar
with the Maharajah and his sons, and had a
variety of sport—tiger, rhino, and leopard. On
the whole he thought Indian shooting overrated.
" It is too civilized. ' To have been tiger-shooting ' always sounded in my ears the same as to
have gone through a battle and run great risks
of one's life. It is not so. The meanest, most
diminutive person might as easily shoot twenty
tigers as the boldest and the fittest. Yet it is worth
a very long journey to see the immense jungle,
the elephants, and all the wild and delightful
surroundings of the Indian forests." He also
reflected a good deal on the difficult question
of the education of Indian princes in England,

and came to the conclusion that Lord Curzon's policy of discouragement was right. On 22nd April he bade a sad farewell to Francis at Bombay, and on 5th May he was dining with Harry Rawlinson, Lord Lovat, and his brother Arthur in London.

Rivy spent most of May in his annual training with the Bucks Yeomanry. In that month of gorgeous weather he greatly enjoyed himself, and in his spare hours he started a polo club in the regiment. For the rest his main interest that summer was polo, and he and his brothers Cecil and Arthur played steadily all the season at Hurlingham and Roehampton. To tell the story of those matches would weary the reader, for of all games polo is the worst subject for the resurrectionist. An arid chronicle of strokes and goals achieved or missed cannot reproduce the glamour of those delectable days. A young man living in London and regularly playing polo recaptures the delights of school time. He is in the pink of bodily health, and, as a background to his work in office or chambers or barracks, has that happy world of greensward and glossy ponies, where of an afternoon and a Saturday he pursues a sport which combines the delicate expertness of the tennis court and the swift excitement of the hunting field. Rivy had a most successful season. " My record," he wrote in September, " is certainly not bad, considering I have only played for three years. I have won the Novice's Cup, the Junior Championship (besides being in the final twice), the Roehampton Cup twice, and the Rugby Open Cup, besides most of the London Handicap Tournaments."

In May Francis attained the desire of his heart and joined the 9th Lancers. Just before leaving he had become very keen on his work with the 60th, and was busy lecturing to his company. " By Jove," he wrote, " soldiering is interesting when you train the men yourself. . . . I think I know Clive nearly by heart, and if only I could get hold of a picture of him, I could imagine him walking about. I lectured the men on him, which they liked very much." At last came the moment of parting.

" I left the regiment on Wednesday, and dined on Tuesday as a guest at a small farewell dinner. I am bound to say when the time came I was most awfully sorry to go. It seemed so funny to think that with the morrow I would be no more a Rifleman, and I fear for a while I became like Amelia and could not restrain the bitter tear. I think they were all sorry I left. It is a consolation to think I leave behind me no regrets, as I have never had words with any one."

A few days later :—

"Here I am, R. G., at last a cavalry soldier, and as happy as any millionaire or cheery bankrupt (whichever of the two is the happiest). I am already attaining the cavalry air—slap my leg, wear spurs with no end of a rattle, and discuss the infantry rather like we Etonians used to talk of the boys at Westminster ! . . . Of course, R. G., I know that I join on most favourable conditions, as all the men and N.C.O.'s have heard about the polo, and about the second day after my arrival every London paper contained an enormous picture of R. G. This has been a great topic here, as all the regiment think it is *me* !

"To-day the farrier-corporal of my troop, who has been shoeing my ponies, said they were the finest lot of cattle he had seen. Then says he, ' You've got a terrible wonderful name for polo in the regiment, sir.' So you see I have joined with trumpets sounding and drums beating, and already I find that my chief difficulty is not from want of feeling at home, but from being too much at home to keep a back seat. However, I mean to keep a back seat until I know my job and have got the measure of all officers."

The Ninth at the time were commanded by Claude Willoughby, who had married Francis's old friend, Miss Sybil Murray of Loch Carron. Francis's squadron leader was Lord Frederick Blackwood. The change woke all his military ambitions. " I am going to try, now I am settled down, for two stages—(1) to be adjutant of this regiment ; (2) to go to the Staff College. . . . I find my four years with the 60th have been an invaluable experience, as I have that confidence which all possess who think they have been taught in a better school. Though I have been here only a fortnight, I find there are several, who are supposed to be teaching me, that I could teach. But I am doing my utmost to keep my mouth shut and learn all I can. The N.C.O.'s and men are first class—a much better class than the infantry. Of course I find the riding chaps superior in the same way as we fox-hunters think the huntsman superior to the gamekeeper. If you can't grasp my meaning, it would take me so much time to explain that you would become weary, so I will leave you in darkness. The difference between the cavalry and the infantry soldier is the same as the difference between Tom Firr or Thatcher and the leading gamekeeper, or between the huntsman of the O.B.H. and Tom Boon. Both, of course, do their work equally well, but one is the nicer to deal with." And at the end he becomes humbler. " By Jove, R. G., I have never appreciated before the good fortune and kindness we receive from the Almighty. Here am I, a good rider and very fond of it, yet I ride only the best horses. But some of the men ! A man is given a horse known to be next door to impossible. Some cannot ride, and are frightened to death. Yet they must ride over the jumps horses that cannot jump, pull and probably run away."

Francis shared a house at Rawal Pindi with

Lord F. Blackwood, and boasted of its comfort, its quiet, and the opulence of its chintzes. He compared it to its advantage with the Bath Club, where Rivy had now gone to live. But in July he found a crumpled leaf in his bed of roses. "R. G., you made 'in theory' to me, some years ago, the observation that it was in the end better to live by oneself and not share a house with a pal. What you said in theory I have been through in practice. Old Freddie has just returned. The first thing I spied among his kit was a gramophone. He turns it on morning, noon, and night. It is quite comical. Old Freddie is one of the best, but he sits, at the age of thirty, the whole day listening to the same old tune, the same old story, the same old 'Bull and Bush.' . . . I am trying to work in spite of the heat, Freddie and his gramophone."

He worked to some purpose. " I must say," he wrote in August, " I like working far more than anything else when I am at it." He stuck steadily to his books, and I find him offering to send Rivy " a clinking book of notes on strategy of Jap. War, *stolen from Lord K*." He was devoted to the Commander-in-Chief, from whom he purloined books. Reggie Barnes * told him of

---

* Now Major-General Sir R. Barnes; commanded the West Lancs
Territorial) Division in France.

Lord Kitchener's methods of work—information which he passed on to Rivy. " He is up at 6 every day, and writes till 8.30 ; then on after breakfast till 2, and then two hours in afternoon. All his correspondence is done by his A.D.C.'s, who typewrite for him—either Fitzgerald, Victor (Brooke), or Reggie ; he never gives anything to a clerk, so that nothing leaks out." In October Lord Kitchener lunched with the Ninth. " I think he likes us awfully. His first remark is always, ' Hullo ! how are the Ninth ? Been killing any more black men ? ' " In the Curzon-Kitchener controversy Francis, of course, took the soldier's side and upheld the military against the civil arm ; but he had a great regard for the new Viceroy, Lord Minto—" a sporting fellow who has ridden three times in the Grand National, and one of the few living who has broken his neck steeplechasing." At the end of October he had the pleasure of informing Rivy that he had come out top in the first part of his examination, and had won a certificate of distinction.

Upon this Francis, who had suffered a good deal from Rivy's scathing comments on his lectures, especially the celebrated one on Clive, thought it was time for him to adopt the rôle of mentor. So he thus addresses his brother :—

"Now for business. What good are you doing in the City ?

"I have been thinking about you and your future prospects for some time, and I have quite come to the opinion that you are wasted hunting for money. In England people are very narrow-minded, and the ruling idea (especially in our family) is that one must be rich.

"I am beginning to think otherwise. To be rich is very nice, but you are no happier, and you do your country no good. Both C. and A. have been successful, but beyond buying extra hunters, deer forests, and houses, to me they have not attained a very high position. I would rather you chucked the City. I think you should enter Parliament and work your way to the Cabinet; I would far rather you succeeded in politics than in the City.

"You know Hugh Cecil, Milner, and Co. They should all give you advice. I hope you will think this over, and that your thoughts will be guided rather by the amount you will help the nation than by the amount with which you will fill your pocket.

"As we stand at present we have not done badly :—

"The Uncle	General
"Uncle Harry . . .	Admiral.
"First Cousin Jack Maxwell	General.
"Harold	Colonel.
"R. G.	Winner of Kadir.
"F. G.	,, ,, Championship.
"Cecil	2nd in National.

"It is about time the City chaps gingered up ! Chuck the City and become Minister of War, and I will get on the Army Council to help you."

To this flattering injunction Rivy replied :—

"You discuss in your letter my future. I, oddly enough,

have been thinking this over for some months. In fact, ever since I've travelled and read I have more and more seen that money is not everything, and my feeling has been politics and not business. But I am convinced of one thing—that the greatest mistake one can make is to go into politics without being exceedingly well furnished, having determined absolutely on your principles, and feeling that you are prepared to back them up with all earnestness, and, so to speak, with your life. Now, many people enter Parliament as Tories because their fathers were Tories, and then find, after some years, that they did not know what Tories and Liberals were, and that their whole sentiments are really Liberal; just as you entered the infantry because your uncle was there, and found later you were born for cavalry.

" I really inwardly don't know whether I am Tory or Liberal, Free Trader or Protectionist, and so I have decided to stay on in the City and earn a good living, but shall not do more work than I find necessary there. I have been fear-fully slack about business in the last six weeks, and read history whenever I got a chance. In this way I hope in about five years to have thoroughly mastered the various opinions and principles of our political leaders, and traced through history how those opinions came to be formed, and discovered whether I agree with them. At the same time I shall have my busi-ness, which will, therefore, make my reading a hobby, and I shall be building up some capital, and shall, if I want to, enter politics well furnished and keen and prepared to join in the contest ; whereas so many people who start politics at twenty-five are bored with them at thirty-three. Chamberlain never entered till he was forty. . . . I shall gradually try to get to know fellows of the Hugh Cecil class, but I want them to see me as an earnest, hard-working chap, not as a stupid stay-at-country-houses-go-to-balls sort of idiot."

Rivy certainly read all that year with praise-worthy persistence. He seems to have found novels a toughish proposition, and generally notes in his diary how he set his teeth and plugged away till he finished one. For example : " I have finished *Vanity Fair*. Read like a Trojan for four days. It is a good book. I never thought Rebecca would turn out such a hot 'un." Burke, on the other hand, had power to make him forget time and place, as witness this entry : " Wednesday I was to have gone to a ball, but after dinner began reading my Burke, and am ashamed to say that I read till 2.45 a.m." In a letter to Francis, in which he made hay of the prose style of that laborious soldier, he bids him have recourse to Burke, "who, though elaborate, is the finest example of the English language." Rivy, indeed, about this time had a curious passion for serious writers, and does not seem to have needed the work on " Concentration " with which Mrs. Cornwallis-West presented him. At Eaton, " where there is a fine but ugly library that no one uses but me," he read *Venus and Adonis*, which he considered " delightful, and fine English." He studied the *Iliad* in Pope's translation, largely during working hours in his City office. " It is a first-class book, full of descriptions of battles, great orations of generals, both before and during a battle, and wonderful deeds of the heroes interested, who slay everybody." He copied extracts from Bacon's *Essays* to send to Francis to point his lectures to his troops. He considered Morley's *Life of Gladstone* " a delightful book " (an epithet almost as unexpected as Raymond Asquith's answer to the stock question as to whether he had read that formidable work ; his reply was, " Often "). At the end of December he mentions that in the previous three months he had got through " history up to 1860 ; *Vanity Fair ;* Homer's *Iliad* (five volumes) ; *Grenville Papers* (three volumes) ; *Life of Macaulay ;* a fair sprinkling of Burke's speeches and his *Life* by Morley ; Shakespeare's *Merchant of Venice* (twice) ; S.'s *Julius Cæsar ; Europe and Asia*, by Townsend ; *Oliver Twist ;* a little of *Childe Harold ;* a book on Napoleon's strategy."

In addition to this miscellaneous reading, he discovered a restless interest in military history, and worked as if he had had the Staff College in prospect. All during the autumn and winter he was coached by Dr. Miller Maguire in the strategy and tactics of famous campaigns—an arrangement in which Francis joined later, and which continued right up to the outbreak of the Great War.

But the " earnest, hard-working chap " was not averse to the country-house visits and balls from which we have seen that he desired his name to be dissociated. On 7th June he writes :—

" Went to a first-class show at Londonderry House. Talk about the Patiala jewels ! One would not have noticed them. The King and Queen and King Alfonso of Spain were there. I got hold of Sybil Grey, who is just back from Canada, and we pushed our way through the people ; stared at kings and queens, elbowed princes, jostled dukes, stepped on mar-quises, ignored earls and generals, and as for commoners we treated them like dirt. It really was capital fun. I found innumerable pals, and had a lot of chaff. The King amused me very much. He is a grand old John Bull, and had a broad grin on his face from beginning to end. The King of Spain is a nice-looking young man of nineteen. I met Miss Whitelaw Reid. Her father has just come over as American Ambassador. He has taken Dorchester House, and I fancy pays about £8,000 a year for it. She said, ' I have not yet explored the whole house, but I guess you could just slide grandly down those stairs on a tea-tray.' "

On 9th June :—

"I met Harry Dalmeny, who amused me very much. What an extraordinary chap he is ! Everybody who plays county cricket sweats blood and goes to bed about 10. Not so Harry. He went to a ball on Friday night and stayed till 3 in the morning. Next day he played against Essex, and knocked up sixty-five runs in about an hour."

On 15th July he was staying at Buckhurst with the Robin Bensons.

" We had a jolly party—Sybil Grey, Miss Brodrick, Paul Phipps, Geoffrey Howard, Douglas Loch and his new wife, and Mr. and Mrs. Asquith, the latter a most charming lady. I asked her how Asquith spent his time, to which she replied by going into the minutest details. She told me he earned £5,000 a year at the Bar (I always thought he earned about £14,000), but he is prohibited by his Parliamentary duties from undertaking certain cases. She told me he lived entirely by rules. He gets up at 8.45, and is at his chambers or in the Courts by 10.30, and works there till 5. He then goes to the House of Commons and stays till 8, when he returns for dinner ; he then goes back to the House till 12. After that, regularly for every day of his life, he reads for two hours. Supposing he goes to a party and does not return till 2, he still sits up and reads for two hours, either his briefs or some serious book, and finishes up with a novel in bed. In discussing certain people she told me that Arthur Balfour was not very well educated in the ordinary sense. I wonder what she would say about you and me, F. G. She would probably compare our brains with an Irishman's whisky bottle—empty."

In August he went to the Westminsters at Eaton for a polo week. The house he thought " the most enormous place I was ever in, but dreadfully ugly, just like the Natural History Museum with two wings added to it." " G. Wyndham (War Minister) came over every day and brought Hugh Cecil. The latter was much interested, and said he ' admired the bravery of the players, while he sat like a miserable weed in a tent.' " In the beginning of September he was in Ireland, staying with Lord Grenfell at the Royal Hospital, and playing a good deal of polo. After that he went to Ashby St. Ledgers to stay with Ivor Guest, where the conversation must have been curious. " Ivor started an argument after dinner which continued for about three and a half hours on : ' Granted that one's time is limited, is it better to read all the masterpieces once and then read them through again, rather than read the masterpieces and then the sidelights referring to them ? ' Ivor argued that a man would do best to read the masterpieces only, whereas Winston and Lytton said it was better to read other books as well, so as to check the masterpieces, for many people learned far more from outside books than from the very highest authorities." There is also this note : " Winston Churchill is undoubtedly exceedingly able, but if you mention a subject to him he instantly must go into an oration. We talked of the Curzon-Kitchener methods. He went into an oration about the Commander-in-Chief being an autocrat, and its danger, etc. By-and-by I discovered that neither Winston nor Ivor had read a word of any of the Blue Books on the subject." From Ashby St. Ledgers he went to Polesden Lacey to stay with Sir Clinton Dawkins, and there he met Lord Milner, who was gradually taking place along with Lord Hugh Cecil as the chief object of his admiration in public life.

In pursuance of the political training which he had laid down for himself, Rivy began that autumn to practise speaking. There was then a great revival of interest in politics in England.

Mr. Balfour's Government was known to be on the eve of resignation, and everywhere caucuses were girding their loins and getting ready for a general election. In spite of his cross-bench professions, Rivy found himself ranging with the Unionists. Most of his friends were of that persuasion ; he was an ardent Imperialist ; he seems to have been a convinced, though imperfectly informed, Tariff Reformer ; and he had strong views on that question of Chinese Labour in South Africa which was to play so sinister a part at the polls. His first adventure in oratory was not very successful. On 18th October he writes in his diary : " Went to a debate at the London School of Economics, and spoke for ten minutes on ' Unpopularity of Railways ' ; was called to order for straying from the subject ; had to read most of my speech." His next attempt was more fortunate. " Attended meeting at Brixton, and spoke for thirty-five minutes on Imperial Responsibilities in South Africa. Biggest attempt I have yet made. Knew the speech so well I hardly had to look at my notes. George Bowles in the chair. Capital fun. A band, and a very jolly evening." He also lectured somewhere on Conscription, and sent his MS. to Francis, who replied thus : " I have read your lecture. What must have struck all who heard it, and what struck me most when I read it, was, how you could have said so much and touched so little on the real subject."

On 5th December, during that uneasy time when Sir Henry Campbell-Bannerman was forming his new Ministry, Rivy went to stay at Hatfield. His account of his visit deserves quotation.

"*Tuesday.*

"A large party, including Asquith and Mrs., Mrs. Laurence Drummond, Etty Grenfell [Lady Desborough], Revelstoke, Lord and Lady Kenmare and Lady Dorothy Browne, General Broadwood, Arthur Strutt, Lady Airlie and Lady Kitty Ogilvie, Dick Cavendish and Lady Moira, Miss Claire Stopford, Edward Packe, Micky Hicks-Beach, Hugh Cecil, and a very nice Miss Asquith. After dinner the older ones played bridge, and we played stupid games like ' snap.' My God! Hugh Cecil did make me laugh; he is the most amusing fellow you ever saw.

"*Wednesday.*

"Most of the party went up to London, except four of us who shot partridges. I should have done better if I had thrown my gun at the birds instead of shooting at them. At dinner I took in Miss Asquith. Afterwards I had a long yarn with Hugh Cecil about politics. We discussed elections and arguing with the working man. He told me that what generally happened was that you visited the working man and employed the finest arguments for about half an hour, and the only reply you got was, ' Oh yes, I quite understand. You have been very well educated, and I don't believe a word you say.' After dinner we did a sort of dumb crambo acting, and I talked politics with Miss Asquith, who is extremely clever and, of course, full of politics.

"In the smoking-room Asquith and H. Cecil discussed the various bishops!

" *Thursday.*

" We went pheasant-shooting. I shot very badly. There were a lot of birds; we got 300. After tea I played bridge against the future Chancellor of the Exchequer. We dressed up for dinner in fancy dress, and had a cotillon afterwards. I went as a toreador.

" I made great pals with Mrs. Asquith. I do not know if you know her, but she is an absolute clinker. She dressed up as a Spanish dancer, and did a *pas seul* before us all. What will people say in about twenty years when they hear this! The leading lady of the Government dancing a *pas seul*, while the Chancellor of the Exchequer looked on! Hugh Cecil said he thought he had dislocated the inner organs of his body from laughter.

" And now for secrets. . . . [Here follow certain matters which have long ago been made public.] Read to-day's *Times*, F. G. There is about half a column on the political situation, which gives you much of what I have written above. Asquith was fearfully perturbed about how they got hold of it, for only six people knew the situation—himself, Grey, Haldane, C.-B., Morley, Tweedmouth, and (proclaim it to your ancestors !) R. G.

" Mrs. Asquith told me that Asquith had had a terrible two days. The Liberals, having been out for ten years, of course owe honours to a great number of people. Innumerable people had called on him and implored him to give them something—men whose whole lives have been given up to working for the party, and now there is nothing for them. This to some of them meant a career finished. So you see that even being Chancellor of the Exchequer and having the making of a Government isn't altogether honey.

" Here is an amusing story of Lady Curzon. The day after Curzon arrived there was a bad accident at Charing Cross. Half the roof fell in, owing to a girder snapping. Lady Curzon said wittily that ' Brodrick must have cut that girder on purpose, but—so like him—was a day late ! '

" Had there not been this crisis, the party at Hatfield was

to have included Austen Chamberlain and Balfour; but they had to stay in London to pack up their belongings. We had great chaff, as Austen C. was packing up to let the Asquiths in. They told me an amusing story that happened last summer. Hugh Cecil and Austen Chamberlain had a race on trays along a gallery. Cecil slipped off his tray and won without it. The judge at the end of the room said, ' The Free Trader has won.' ' Yes,' says Cecil, ' but he has lost his seat in doing it ! ' "

In the same letter Rivy gives Francis a piece of advice most characteristic of the attitude of both the Twins to life. They were devotees of the " grand manner," which appears to do things easily and without effort, however much laborious spade-work may be done in secret. Francis is adjured to study the hill tribes against a possible frontier campaign in the next two years. " Do not tell anybody what you are about. For some reason or other people are always inclined to think a person who does anything from instinct more wonderful than if he has practised at it first ; just as you hear, ' Isn't it wonderful how So-and-so plays polo so well, and never practises at all ? '—whereas, as a matter of fact, the said person has been years practising. Demosthenes was renowned for his impromptu speeches. In reality, he had an underground chamber full of looking-glasses, where he used to rehearse every single speech that he made—for weeks, and sometimes years."

CHAPTER IV.

1906–1907.

To Rivy, as to most people in England, the absorbing question in the first months of 1906 was politics. Seeing a fight approaching, he conceived it his duty to hurl himself into the thick of it. He had lessons in elocution, and discovered that he breathed badly ; so he promptly had his adenoids removed, and, a little later, a broken bone taken from his nose. When convalescent he went to stay at Eaton with the Duke of Westminster, who had returned that morning from South Africa. There he found a large party, and had some good shooting and hunting. " Imagine the change of times. The meet was twenty-six miles away, and formerly they had to catch the 8.50 train, and did not get back until 9 at night. Yesterday Bend Or and I and John Fowler, with Bend Or driving, went in a new motor car he had just bought of 100 horse-power that could go ninety miles an hour. It certainly frightened the life out of me. We were supposed to start at

10, but started at 10.25, and arrived first at the meet at 10.55. . . . Wilfred Ricardo was in fine form. He made me roar at breakfast one morning, when, owing to his not having a horse, he was going out snipe-shooting. ' To think—ah—that I—ah—am forty years old and have never shot a snipe! I feel the same sort of sensation that these big-game shooters must know when they are approaching the tracks of a rhino.' "

After that, in Rivy's phrase, " everything was elections."

" I thought it a rare chance, so have been hard at it. On Monday I went to a meeting of 1,500 beyond King's Cross. The Conservative candidate spoke, but they booed and shouted and yelled to such an extent that he had to give it up, and I did not speak. Five were chucked out. Such remarks as these : ' Hold your jaw!' ' Shut your mouth!' ' Chuck him out!' ' Where's Joey?' ' Pigtails!' amused me much. Tuesday another meeting at Bow, in the East End. Much more quiet. The candidate spoke so long and was asked so many questions that I only spoke about six minutes. Wednesday went down to Enfield, in Essex, and found a huge meeting of 2,000. Felt in the deuce of a funk for a minute. There was a perpetual uproar of ' No Chinese!' ' Pigtail!' etc. The candidate spoke for three-quarters of an hour, and then they howled him down. Then R. G. spoke for twenty minutes amid a continual roar. I had to wait half this time while they yelled at me. Rare good fun. On such occasions one is not a bit nervous, only pining for them to stop and then give them hell. The speaker after me began : ' Ladies and gentlemen ' (roars)—' Gentlemen' (roars)—' Gentlemen and others ' (laughter and uproar). After interruption—

' One thing is very sure : if they tax brains you'll get rich.'
Thursday evening went down to Aylesbury, and motored
seven miles from there to a village and spoke on Chinese
Labour for thirty-five minutes. They were perfectly quiet ;
only two interruptions, both of which I sat on."

The next week he went to Woolwich, where he
had a rough time with Chinese Labour. "They
kept interrupting me and yelling that they considered the black man to be every bit as good as
the white man. To which I replied : ' Would
you allow your daughters to marry black men ? '
' Of course we would,' they all shouted. That
pretty well knocked me out." Two days later he
went to Loughton, in Essex, where he had a real
success. " Just as the meeting began they gave
me a few points that had been raised, and asked
me to deal with them. I got in the deuce of a
funk and thought I was certain to make a mess
of it. Luckily, the points that were raised were
such as I knew pretty well and could fit into my
speech without very much altering the trend of
my arguments. I spoke for three-quarters of an
hour without faltering, and was never interrupted.
Afterwards there were some Radicals there who
asked me questions, and I had to answer them on
the spur of the moment. Luckily again, I knew
their points, and was able to score off them,
which made things even better." The result of

the elections Rivy took in a philosophical spirit.
His chief grievance was that so many of his " pals
have been chucked; on the other hand, Helms-
ley, Dalmeny, and Thomas Robartes got in."

Meantime Francis was happy and busy in his
new regiment. He changed to David Campbell's squadron, and was hoping soon to be pro-
moted Captain. His letters show that he was
very satisfied with life—his friends, his work,
his house, and his prospects. It was the time of
the Prince of Wales's tour, and at Christmas he
was engaged in the special manœuvres arranged
in honour of the visit, his division being commanded by Douglas Haig. There he met innumerable old friends, and his letters home are
chiefly lists of names. He kept open house at
Rawal Pindi, and entertained the officers of the
60th and various German attachés, besides an
occasional English lady. He described the manœuvres in a long letter to his uncle, Lord
Grenfell, which Rivy was good enough to admit
was written in better English than usual.

" To all soldiers the organization was wonderful. Lord K.
refused any rehearsal of any sort. On Wednesday night the
Northern Army was thirty-five miles away—marching and
fighting from 8 p.m. to 2.30 a.m. On Thursday at 10, 60,000
troops were fighting hard twenty-three miles from Pindi.
At 7 on Friday morning the whole, having slept in their
various camps round Pindi, and having cast their khaki, were

paraded in tunics, with spotless clothes and with shining
buttons. By 3.30 p.m. on that day the great review was over
without a hitch of any sort or kind. And yet they say the
British officer is a fool and knows nothing ! One squadron
only of the 3rd Hussars appeared in khaki, some of their
transport having been delayed. This, to my mind, is wonderful, and no one who has seen the transport out here, with
the thousands of camels, mules, carts, ponies that 60,000
troops require, can but be amazed. It must be remembered
that individually not one native servant or driver knows who
he is or where he is going, and yet 60,000 troops were concen-
trated that night without difficulty."

Francis gave up his rôle of host with regret.
" I quite miss them," he wrote. " The chances
a soldier gets of living under the same roof as a
woman are few and far between in this country.
I felt quite homely with ladies under my roof and
larky maids picketed in the garden."

When it was all over he went off to Calcutta
to a polo tournament, where Francis Scott, who
was on the Viceroy's staff, introduced him to the
Mintos. There he met Harry Rawlinson and
consulted him about his next step. He had been
offered a post on Lord Kitchener's staff, and was
for some days in a state of indecision. Finally
he refused it. " It is a question of chucking the
regiment now and going on the staff, or becoming
an adjutant and then going to the Staff College.
The latter is far soundest." He, however, settled
with Victor Brooke that if serious war broke out

on the frontier he would be allowed to go there, and he arranged with Lord Burnham that if the affair were only a small campaign he would go as *Daily Telegraph* correspondent. In the intervals between polo and discussions about his career he found time to go over a jute mill and send Rivy a lengthy description of the process ; to pump a German officer, Count Krage of the Headquarters Staff, on the German Army system ; and to take his full share in the gaieties of Calcutta. " In the evening I went to a State ball, and enjoyed it very much indeed. Danced in a circle set apart for P. Wales, and so found no crush ! What a nice girl Harry Crichton's is ! By Jove ! R. G., these ladies do look different to the old trouts out here. We had quite a family supper party—Francis Scott, Lady Eileen [Elliot], Harry and his lady, and Mrs. Derek Keppel."

At the end of January he was back at Rawal Pindi, where he became the hero of a celebrated adventure. I quote his laconic narrative.

" I went to a domino dance. Douglas Compton, Freddie [Blackwood], and I dined alone with a bottle of pop. I went dressed up by Lady Blood as a woman. Capital fun, especially as Freddie defied me to go into the ladies' dressing-room. When the ' Take off masks ' sounded, with about sixty women I went into the dressing-room, where they were all powdering their noses. All went well until the time arrived when I was the only one left masked. Some girl came up and said, ' Who is it ? I believe it's a man.' She then started out to find her mamma, and I started out to find the door. For days afterwards all Pindi rang with this scandal. A man in the ladies' dressing-room ! The story I heard, as told in our mess, was this : ' A man went into the ladies' dressing-room, and found all the ladies undressing. One lady saw it was a man, gave a yell, and fainted. All the ladies then dashed at the man to tear his clothes off ; he, however, flew for the door, pursued by furious women, and just escaped. All the husbands are now looking for the man, and everybody is saying what they would do with him if they caught him.' I agreed with everybody that it was dashed bad form, and could not think who it could be."

But he was busy with other things than such escapades. He employed a coach to come to him twice a week for military history, and he entertained a German cavalry officer, Count Königsmarck, from whom he learned much that was faithfully recorded in his diary. He was also working hard at Hindustani for his examination. In March his polo team won the Inter-Regimental Cup in the Subalterns' Tournament, and in April he went on leave on a trip to the frontier. " A capital chap, Howell of the Intelligence, is arranging my show," he told Rivy. " Remember Howell's name. One day you will see him General, Sir or Lord—a mighty clever varmint." *

* Brigadier-General Philip Howell was killed in Aveluy Wood during the Battle of the Somme.

I have before me Francis's journal of his frontier tour. He started from Peshawur on the 11th of April, and travelled by Kohat and Bannu, followed the Afghan border line, and penetrated some distance into Waziristan. The diary is a vigorous narrative, but most of the reflections on frontier policy are now out of date. The writer was especially uneasy about Russia, and has much to say about the Muscovite strategic railways. After his fashion he intersperses many good stories. One is of a certain border chief who possessed a small cannon and only one bullet. Whenever he saw his enemy from the top of a tower he used to let the cannon go. The enemy, having to pass the tower most days to go to work, used to pick up the bullet, and every now and then an intermediary was sent to buy it back for two shillings! The document was sent to Rivy, who remonstrated on Francis's carelessness. " You must really send your letters in stronger envelopes. You say, ' Treat these papers as most confidential,' and yet they appear to have come • to pieces and to have been put into an envelope by the Post Office."

In May Francis was back at Murree, very anxious about his English leave, since the 9th Lancers were under orders for South Africa. He hoped to get it in October before sailing, and

be in England for the winter. At home he proposed to do three things—to learn German and
study Germany, to go over the Franco-German
battle-fields, and to do a course of topography at
Chatham. A long letter from Harry Rawlinson
in June advised France instead of Germany, and
comforted Francis on the sore subject of the
transfer to South Africa on the ground that the
dangerous state of affairs among the Natal natives
would probably soon lead to a native rebellion.
A letter from Francis to Rivy about this time is
typical of the writer, who was passionately generous provided his virtues could escape notice. " I
am so grateful to you for making me some cash,
and I have been able to put it to good use. Our
riding master, K.—such a good chap—could not
afford to bring his wife and two children to the
hills for the summer, so I have taken a house
for him. It cost about £50, but it was well
worth it. You have no idea how awful it is for
women, and especially children, in Pindi in the
hot weather. Please treat this as *entre nous* and
tell no one else. K.'s letter of gratitude is really
due to you, for if it was not for you I would be
begging myself."

In June Francis went in for his examination
in Hindustani, which he passed with honour,
and then departed for a short trip in Kashmir.

The rest of the summer was rather poisoned for him by a row which he had in July with a native pleader, who ventured to race him on a dusty road in a tonga, and was summarily called over the coals for his pains. The pleader brought an action against Francis for assault, and was emboldened by the behaviour of the military authorities, who foolishly tried to persuade him to keep it out of court. For a few weeks Francis was a prominent figure in the native press— " this brutal lieutenant, who is a son of a lord and a friend of the King's," etc. The situation was a delicate one, for the 9th Lancers had once before got into similar trouble. Francis, knowing that Lord Kitchener wished the thing not to come to trial, and desirous to obey his chief, was yet most unwilling to climb down when he believed he had a good case, and in the end managed to effect a satisfactory settlement to the credit of both parties. This gave him an occasion to expound to Rivy his philosophy of life. " I have been guided by a few principles: (1.) Form your own opinions and never mind other people's. (2.) Keep to the truth and have it out. It has always beaten lies and liars. (3.) What is done is done, and no amount of regrets and groanings can undo it ; so make the best of a bad job. (4.) Make sound dispositions, and leave the rest to fortune. (5.) Deal with natives by deeds rather than by entreaties."

Rivy, when his electioneering was over, went to hospital for a slight operation, and two days later rose from his couch to go to the House of Lords to hear Lord Milner on Chinese Labour. He was busy with discursive reading, principally Pope's *Odyssey* and Disraeli's *Lord George Bentinck*—" also a topping book entitled *The Education of an Orator*, by Quintilian, which is a translation. It discusses the whole of one's education from the age of about four, and tells you the best books to read, how to learn to discuss and argue, etc. What made me get it was that in Gladstone's *Life* I found continual allusions to it, and also in Macaulay." A little later we find that earnest politician in the House of Commons under the Gallery. " In the evening Joe and Balfour had a rare crack at the Government. A fellow called Smith * made what is said to be one of the best maiden speeches for the past twenty years. He spoke for an hour, and kept the whole place in roars of laughter. Even in the report in the *Times* it appears amusing. You must imagine a very sarcastic voice, and each time the Ministers cheered he gave them a whack in the mouth

* Now Lord Birkenhead, Lord Chancellor of England.

with some snub. I never enjoyed anything better."

Rivy felt the shades of the prison house beginning to close about him. A proof was that he was more amused by politics than by racing. Here is his reflection upon the Grand Military : " I can remember thinking the fellows who rode at Sandown most wonderful heroes, whereas on Saturday it struck me that there were some rather moderate jockeys flogging round on very moderate horses." But youth revived in May when, after doing a Yeomanry course at Netheravon under Reggie Barnes, he began his polo season. He generally played with his brother Cecil, and the combination was highly successful. This kind of sentence occurs constantly in his letters : " R. G. has never been in such form since he played polo. He got five goals—two runs down half the length of the field and one down the whole length, and a goal at the end of each." But his letters did not please the exile in India. " You never mention the family doings," Francis expostulated, " or the gossip or scandal of the town. I see in a paper Lady Warwick is a Socialist. You never told me. Write news, R. G.—not *Times* articles, as I take in the *Mail*. I always understood the advantage of a shorthand typist was the amount they could write and their powers against fatigue.

I recommend the sack of yours, as he seems to own neither of these qualities."

In June Rivy changed his business. He had met Mr. Bonbright in America, and he now went into partnership in an English branch of his house, of which the directors were Lord Fairfax, Mr. Fisher, and himself. His agreement entitled him to twenty-five per cent. of the profits, and at the moment the prospects seemed rosy. Francis received the news gravely. " Well done, R. G. It does seem funny : you a £4,000-a-year johnnie and F. G. a £400-a-year-in-debt chap. You deserve all you have got. But don't become a miser, or selfish, and think it necessary that you should spend it all on yourself. You can help our pals royally."

The letters of the brothers that summer are amusing reading. Francis, busy with work for examinations and doleful about his leave, took up a critical attitude to life. He saw faults in his colleagues which he had not noticed before ; one he described with startling insight as " the sort of chap who gets up things on board ship." But he was also slightly critical of Rivy. " Thanks awfully for the evening waistcoats," he wrote. " Did you see them before they started ? I asked you for the latest fashion ! The ones you have sent I know when I left England were beginning to get out of date in Putney!" Rivy, indeed, that summer was in a somewhat schoolmasterly mood. Francis, a little bored with slogging at Hindustani, asked for an occasional novel—something that would be " a relief at night and would ginger one up for the history books." He mildly suggested some book like *Mademoiselle de Maupin*. Rivy replied by sending him that gloomy work, *The Jungle*, and advising him if he wanted anything more to read *Pickwick* again. " Windham Baring told me his father [Lord Cromer] always rereads these old books, and so what you hear him quote is only some joke he has read a hundred times." He added the recommendation that Boswell's *Johnson* and Macaulay's *Life* were books that Francis should always be reading in his spare moments. A week later he gave him his philosophy of reading.

" Do please give up reading rubbishy novels. There are books that have survived the criticism of centuries ; surely these must be more worth reading than worthless stuff that lasts about three weeks. Such books as Walpole's *Letters*, Shakespeare's *Plays*, Boswell's *Johnson*, Macaulay's *Life*, Lecky's *History*, Morley's *Miscellanies*, and even Morley's *Gladstone* are all things that are easy to read and will profit you ten thousand times more than what you call ' light reading.' I advise you to send a telegram to Calcutta and ask them to send you a cheap copy of Shakespeare or Walpole's *Memoirs*, and read them. If on the receipt of this you wish me to pick out ten or twelve books of the above sort, well

Francis at Polo.

bound, and send them out, let me have a cable reading ' Good books.' Or if you still want me to send rubbishy novels, send a cable reading ' Novels.' "

As Rivy then proceeded to give a long account of a dinner with Leonard Brassey, a ball at the Ritz, and the final of the Handicap Tournament at Hurlingham, Francis may have felt that his mentor scarcely did justice to his innocent desire for a little variety in life. " I am honestly played out in this country," he wrote, " and now hate everything. We are existing, not living. I long for a dart in England or France. . . . You see, R. G., out here one is rather run down and sometimes depressed. The hot weather and all its discomforts are raging. Last year I slept in the day, but this year I am fighting it. One can read a stiff book for a certain time every day, but a punkah swinging backwards and forwards and creaking and squeaking, together with a temperature of over 100 degrees, drives one either to sleeping or to an exciting book in an armchair." And he went on to explain that he was satiated with the *History of Cavalry* by Denison, and wanted " such books as the *Life of Madame de Pompadour*, or Napoleon as a *man*, naming the women as well as the countries he captured."

With his departure in prospect he wished to give presents to his friends, and especially to the

Bloods. For Sir Bindon he suggested a good sporting book with pictures of " lions seizing goats, lions springing on donkeys, etc." But Rivy would have none of it. He was determined that Sir Bindon should have a " really well-written book," and suggested " *The Life of Chatham*, Walpole's *Letters*, or, still better, Plato's *Republic.*" Small wonder that Francis began to fear that his brother's culture was becoming too much for him.

In September everything changed. Francis Scott invited him to Simla to stay with the Mintos, and life was once again rosy. " By Jove, R. G., this *is* a holiday. Here I am in a house *with stairs*, and built like an English country house. I could only gasp for two days. One is simply taken aback by the niceness of these people. Lord Minto is the best, after the Uncle, I ever met. He is full of stories, and loves talking of racing and forgetting he is Viceroy. The other day he said, ' I always wish I had been a trainer.' Can you picture any other Viceroy saying that ? . . . It is a great business getting the Ameer to come here. Formerly he had always flatly refused. But the Viceroy wrote him such a kind, friendly letter that he said he felt it his duty to please so great a gentleman."

He spent a happy week at Simla in the com-

pany of the Viceroy and Lady Minto and the
daughters, who were reverentially known throughout India as "the Destroying Angels." "After
tea we all rode—His Ex., Lady M., Francis, and I.
The two girls, Lady Ruby and Lady Violet, ride
astride. We galloped like blazes down the roads.
The girls made me, as they go like hello. I went
for a long ride with Lady Violet. She is a master
on her horse ; drives a coach, etc. ; at the same
time loves music, art, etc., and hates men. There
is a cup here for gymkhanas, held weekly, for the
lady who wins most events. She was second;
Lady Eileen third. She said, ' Father was simply
beaming all over last night after you talked to him ;
he came home and said, " I must put our boy in
that regiment." ' . . . His Ex. told us stories
of Indians, his trips in the wilds, cock-fighting,
prize-fighting, etc.—how he took Jem Mace to
Harrow and backed him against ' Bottles.' Lady
M. begged me to try and find her some chaps for
their staff. It is a pretty difficult job, for every
one falls in love with the girls. . . . I rode home
with Francis, and we bucked of old days. We are
determined to have you out, and your books in the
fire. I hear you have become a sort of heavy-
handed old man. You had better drop that when
I return. We'll go back three years then, give
the books a holiday, and enjoy life." That visit

to Simla was the beginning for Francis of a close friendship with Lady Minto, who had given him a new insight into the problems of British rule in India. He continued to correspond with her and to expound his views on administration. " I have just written a long letter to Lady Minto, begging her not to worry what India thought of their rule, for it was so difficult to judge a ruler. Time always alters opinions." And he gave as an example the somewhat disparate cases of Warren Hastings, the Duke of Wellington, and Mrs. Fitzherbert! The life of the last-named lady was one of the few lighter books which Rivy had allowed him.

Francis arrived in South Africa towards the end of October, and was presently settled with the regiment at Potchefstroom. The immediate result was a fit of profound depression. Potchefstroom is a pleasant little town in a green, well-watered valley, but after India it appeared comfortless and the life dull. South Africa seemed the home of senseless extravagance. As he wrote to Lord Grey : " You cannot realize the terrible expenses incurred here for merely living. We spend four times what we spent in India, and get no return whatever." The country, too, at the moment was suffering from severe financial depression, which intensified the gloom. There were other drawbacks.

"We have been given some terrible horses for this regiment," Francis wrote. "They hardly represent what the richest nation should give its best regiment. We are quite ashamed, as we own all sorts except cavalry horses." On the last day of the year, in a letter to Rivy, he summarized his annual record with some melancholy. "I fear I have done little to advance myself and improve my brain powers. A visit to the frontier, a language, one big polo tournament, a first-class row, and the departure from India are the main things I have done." He cheered up a little after beating the 4th Hussars at polo by six goals to two when the Ninth had only nine ponies and their six best polo players on leave. But the bright spot on his horizon was his leave, which was due in the beginning of the new year.

Meantime Rivy had been living a strenuous life. He rushed out to South Africa in August for a short visit, and was back again in October. In November he was at Hatfield, learning wisdom from Hugh Cecil, which he duly recorded for his brother's advantage, and making a speech at the United Service Institution which earned him a letter of thanks from Sir Robert Baden-Powell. On the 16th of that month he started with his brother Arthur for Mexico, the party including Arthur's wife, Lady Victoria, and his sister, Mrs. Bulteel.

An assiduous study of Prescott's *Conquest of Mexico* on the voyage was his preparation for the country, and in the few weeks there he certainly managed to achieve a considerable variety of experiences. His cousin, Mr. Max-Muller, was at the Embassy, and through his agency the party had an interview with President Diaz. His reading during his stay is characteristic in its catholicity—" *Kim*, the Travels of St. Paul in the Bible, and some of *Paradise Lost*." Early in January the party were with the Greys at Government House, Ottawa, where Lady Victoria was suddenly taken ill with typhoid, contracted in Mexico. Rivy was eager to be home to meet Francis on his arrival in England, but felt bound to stay in Ottawa. " Without me old Arthur is practically alone. Besides this, the Greys have no relations here except strange A.D.C.'s, and it is a relief, I think, to them to feel they have some one on Arthur's side to keep him company and cheer him up. Mate, I would give a thousand pounds to have met you on your arrival and gone with you and shown you all the changes since you left. I feel fearfully sick at the idea of any one meeting you before me. . . . Ernest is to be your valet until we get another good one ; I can get the Bath Club valet to look after me when you take him anywhere. I have told him to get your room ready and put flowers there and make it comfortable. Tell him to put some of my pictures there also, and to get my sitting-room straight for you. Remember it is to be your home. . . . Don't go and see my office or partners till I get back. In fact, F. G., I feel terribly sick at your seeing any one or being told anything about the family doings except by R. G."

Francis arrived on February 9, 1907, but Rivy was not there to meet him. Arthur's young wife did not rally from her fever, and died on 3rd February. It was the first time for long that death had entered the family, and it was a sober and saddened Rivy that returned to rejoin his brother in that communal London life to which they had so joyfully looked forward.

CHAPTER V.

1907–1909.

THE Twins were now twenty-six years old, and, as they had grown more easily distinguishable in person, so they had developed idiosyncrasies in character. Francis remained of the two the younger in mind. He took his soldiering very seriously, but for him the Service was a kind of enlarged Eton—a thing with its own standards and taboos, offering certain definite ambitions in work and sport, which enabled him to lead a full and satisfying life without questionings. He was never in doubt about the values of things — he took them for granted ; whereas Rivy was for ever at the business of stock-taking. Francis had sometimes an uncanny power of going to the heart of a matter, but usually he accepted life as it came. Rivy was a more perplexed soul. His vision was wider than his brother's, but more often confused. Both had immense high spirits, but Rivy had moments of real bewilderment and depression. He was apt to feel himself on the fringes of life when he longed to be at the centre, and since his thirst was habitually deeper than his brother's, it was less readily quenched.

On another side the two were like the scriptural Martha and Mary. Long ago Rivy had made up his mind that he was Francis's protector and guardian, and he laboured to make money, not for himself, but that his brother might never be stinted. That brother, as careless of cash as the lilies in the field, went whistling on his cavalier course, while Rivy knit his brows and laboured to increase their joint resources. In every circumstance he thought first of Francis—his comfort, his education, his career ; and, without a touch of priggishness, subordinated every plan to this end. He never dreamed that he was doing anything unusual, so great was his fraternal pride. He had chosen for himself what seemed to him the natural and inevitable rôle of the prosaic brother of a phœnix. He was teaching himself, a civilian in a sedentary business, the first lesson of the soldier— subordination ; and he learned it, I think, more perfectly than Francis. The difference appeared in their polo. Rivy was one of the steadiest players in England, never working for individual show but only for the game—a sober exponent of team-work. Francis was always incalculable, and sometimes fantastically bad ; but on his day he could be marvellous—a thunderbolt, a tornado, a darting flame.

The year 1907 is a lean one for the Twins' biographer. They were both at home, and so free from the necessity of correspondence. Rivy came back from Canada on 16th February to find Francis in London, and the two set themselves to console their brother Arthur in his bereavement. They collected an excellent lot of ponies, and the whole summer was devoted to polo, except for a course which Francis went through at the Cavalry School at Netheravon, where he began to work seriously for the Staff College. Rivy took enormous pains with his grooms and stablemen. He got beds from Heal for them to sleep in, and used to provide sumptuous teas for them after a successful match.

The brothers got together a polo team known as the Freebooters, in which Rivy was No. 2, Francis No. 3, and the Duke of Roxburghe back. Originally Cecil Grenfell was No. 1, but his place was afterwards taken by Captain Jenner, the joint polo manager at Ranelagh. This team won the Hurlingham Championship Cup, beating Roehampton (a team mainly composed of the brothers Nickalls) by four goals to two. That season established the fame of the Grenfell family on the polo field. I do not propose to describe the details of

RIVY ON "CINDERELLA."

those old contests, but room must be found for a letter of Rivy's telling of the greatest match of the season, England against Ireland, played at Dublin in Phœnix Park. The Irish team was : Major Rotherham, the Hon. Aubrey Hastings, Captain Hardress Lloyd, and Mr. P. P. O'Reilly. For England there played Rivy, Captain H. Wilson, Mr. Pat Nickalls, and Captain Matthew-Lannowe. England won by six goals to five, and Rivy had the satisfaction of hitting the winning goal. Here is his account :—

" There was a strong wind blowing down the ground which I think much spoilt the game. At times it was very slow and sticky—I think partly from the polo being so high class and each fellow stopping the other one hitting out. The ball continually hit a pony in the hock and bounded out, and we were several times stopped for accidents.

" I rode ' Cinderella ' the first ten, and the dodger ' Despair ' the second. Got away on the latter about mid-field, and, evading all opposition, got the first goal on the near side amid applause from the Saxons. Shortly afterwards Rotherham did a characteristic run down and scored amid yells from the Irish. The third ten I rode Roxburghe's pony, which played fairly well, though he wants to be taught to jump off quicker. The fourth ten ' Cinderella,' who played magnificently : I got another goal on her at a difficult angle, and made two or three good runs. Pat (Nickalls) got two goals, and gave us a lead of four to two. Hardress then got a very good goal ; the Irish threw their hats in the air all round the ground. Rotherham then got away and got another goal ; you never heard such cheering in your life ! In the fifth ten I got away on ' Despair ' and went all down the ground, but somehow missed an absolute sitter. I think the wind affected the flight of the ball, as it only missed by inches. We then got a fifth and sixth: the latter was not allowed, as Bertie Wilson fell as the ball was hit and hurt his knee. The other side then got a fifth, and three minutes before time in the last chukker, in which I rode 'Cinderella,' I got a sixth, and so won the match. It was a pretty uncomfortable moment. Bertie Wilson cantered into the middle of the ground; 'Cinderella' turned like lightning, and I found myself forty yards in front of everybody. If I hit the goal, there was no glory; if I missed it, probably fearful abuse. Luckily I just snicked it through. I enjoyed the match very much indeed; it was such fun hearing those Irish chaps yelling the whole time."

In August and September Arthur was at Howick with his children, and the Twins stayed there. Lord Hugh Cecil was among the visitors, and Rivy had the felicity of bringing Francis to sit at his feet. The City that year can have seen little of Rivy, and politics knew him not; indeed, I gravely doubt whether his books left their shelves. He had his brother beside him, and was bent on enjoying life. As soon as the season began they hunted together, and early in December Francis had a smash and broke his collar bone. The two went to the Duke of Westminster at Eaton for Christmas, and while there took part in an escapade which enjoyed for a day or two a wide notoriety. One evening after dinner the Duke suggested motoring, as the weather was clear and cold, and proposed going over to Cholmondeley Castle, where there had been some talk of a dance. Arrived at the Castle, they could get no reply to their ringing of the bell. The place stood silent and apparently untenanted, except that on the ground floor a window had been left open through which came the reflection of a bright fire. It was like a scene in a play, and the spirit of melodrama entered into the party. They crawled through the window, groped their way down a passage, and found themselves in the dining-room. It was empty, but all the lights were still burning, the sideboards gleamed with plate, and in the centre of the table stood a massive race cup which Lord Cholmondeley had won and which he valued highly. As they had come a long way to find no dancing or any other entertainment, the devil of mischief possessed them, and they resolved to carry off the cup as a token of the visit, and return it next day. So they put a bit of coal in the cup's place, and departed as silently as they had come. In leaving the lodge gates the car swerved against a pillar, thereby leaving a clue to the fugitives.

There had been many burglaries about that time, and when the owner discovered that the cup had gone he was naturally excited, and telephoned at once to Scotland Yard. As bad luck would have it, the party turned up late next morning at the meet, and the Duke did not get

an opportunity of speaking to Lord Cholmondele .
But from the rest of the field they heard hig -
coloured accounts of the outrage—how Scotla d
Yard was hot on the trail of the motor-car ga g,
who had fortunately damaged their car on he
Castle gate-post. Somewhat later in the day he
Duke found a chance of explaining the t ing
to Lord Cholmondeley, who took it in exce ent
part and was much relieved to know tha the
cup was safe. But the wheels of the law, nce
set in motion, could not easily be stayed. For
days detectives were scouring Cheshire, exan ning
every garage for traces of a maimed ca and
the popular press in startling headlines to d the
tale of the great burglary. It was a sad blow
to lovers of sensation when the matter w suddenly dropped and only a scanty explanat n was
forthcoming.

In April 1908 Francis returned to Sou Africa
after winning the United Hunts Point o-Point
Race at Melton. He took with him French
tutor to assist him in acquiring the Frenc tongue,
for he was by way of working steadil for the
Staff College. To show his linguistic progress
he occasionally sent Rivy letters written in a very
tolerable imitation of the language o Molière.
The year in England had enormously refreshed

him and prepared him to make the best of South
Africa, and his first letters from Potchefstroom
were very contented.

"Everything here has improved beyond recognition. I
never saw a place so much improved in a year. Every one
seems pleased to see me again. In fact, R. G., the regiment is
A1, not a single stiff here at present. I quite forgot how happy
I am with the regiment. I have so many interests, I love the
soldiering, like polo, and love my books. I never knew I had
so many—I have had to have two new bookcases made."

His first trouble on his return was with a batch
of ponies which Rivy had bought in Canada the
previous year, and which by some blunder had
been sent straight to South Africa instead of to
England, where the Twins could have seen them
and judged them. They proved perfectly useless,
and most of them were sent home for Rivy to
sell. Francis resumed his polo with great energy,
and complained to his brother that he was an in-
different member of a very fine team. He found
it hard to work with his tutor, however, principally from lack of time. " Some days I do five
hours and the next one. To-day, for instance, 7 to
12 at the range in the hot sun ; 12 to 1.30 in
stables. I tried to do one hour with him after
lunch, but felt so knocked out I had to stop."
Both brothers had compiled elaborate note-books
of polo tips in England ; both had irretrievably

lost them, and each accused the other. Francis
records an Eton dinner on the 4th June with Lord
Methuen in the chair, after a football match in
which Mr. D. O. Malcolm, Lord Selborne's
private secretary, distinguished himself. He was
shown by his colonel his confidential report,
which he paraphrased as follows : " This officer
is fit to be an adjutant. He is a very hard-working
officer and has very great application. He is
anxious to work for the Staff College, for which
he is well suited. He is not fit at present, as he
has been away from his regiment at Netheravon
for about a year. He is not brilliant, but very
ambitious. He has tact and a Good Temper.
(What Ho !) He lacks ballast at present, but this
will come, and then I expect great things of him."

At the end of June he went to Bloemfontein
for a polo tournament, and the 9th Lancers, who
for the last six years had either won or been in
the final of every tournament they played in, were
soundly beaten by the 4th Dragoon Guards. The
disaster sent Francis with renewed zest to his
books. " I have been working like an absolute
tiger this week. It is wonderful the amount one
can do when one can live for it and has got
nothing else to think of. I cannot stop thinking
about what I have been reading. The result is
that it affects my sleep a good deal, and I take a

long time to go to sleep. I am certain if I worked like this for six months I should either get into Hanwell or into the Staff College, and not merely qualify. I sometimes feel worn out and long to chuck it, but in my heart of hearts I really love it." About this time, too, he began to acquire a restless interest in Germany. He was always asking his twin about German finances, and whether she could afford the expense of a big war.

Meantime Rivy had been the target of fortune. His disasters began almost as soon as Francis left. On 16th April, while cantering his pony "Despair," she suddenly reared and fell back on him, and the pommel of the saddle caught him in the pelvis. He was taken to St. Thomas's Hospital, where his pelvis proved to be intact, but a muscle was badly lacerated. In the hospital he seems to have enjoyed himself.

" On Sunday morning we have Communion at 6.45 a.m. I could not help being vastly amused. The old chaplain read the prayers very quietly so as not to be too noisy, whereas in every cubicle were fellows, some with no insides, some with insides that had just been sewn up, and about five groaning and gasping for breath. Throughout the service the parson walked from bed to bed on tiptoe ; quite unnecessary, considering the noise the patients were making. . . . There were about ten dashed pretty nurses, who told me about the patients they had had in the theatre. One of them told me that they had absolute proof that three hours' sleep before midnight was worth four after. The man who goes to bed at 9 and gets up at 4.30

can work tremendously hard without any ill effects for years, whereas late-hour workers must knock off after a while. She gave as an example Society people, who always have to go to watering-places after the season, also M.P.'s ; whereas nurses, surgeons, and lawyers can go plodding on. I shall try to go to bed early before big polo matches."

He also made friends with an eminent Lambeth burglar who had two broken legs from having been pitched out of a house by an athletic curate. As Rivy felt almost a professional after his experience at Cholmondeley Castle, the two became confidential and exchanged reminiscences.

The next piece of bad luck was the sale of Francis's ponies at Tattersall's, which fetched very poor prices. For several weeks Rivy's thigh was weak, and the appalling weather in early May made polo nearly impossible. He then went for his Yeomanry training at Stowe Park. He found great difficulties in getting together a good polo team that summer, and was persistently unlucky with his horse-coping. On the last Saturday in May he was playing in the match of the Roehampton team against the Rest of England, when he had a really bad accident.

" In the fourth ten I got clean away, but did not get my drive quite straight. I therefore had to make a hook drive, which went straight in front of goal. Lloyd and I were each going at somewhat of an angle. In stretching out to make a near-side stroke I think he just tipped my pony's quarters ; anyhow I lost my balance and fell in front of 'Sweetbriar,' who seemed to peck over. She also seemed to have eight legs, and all legs struck various parts of my body, two of them on the head. I am not sure whether she stepped on my ankle or twisted the spur. Anyhow, it at once hurt like blazes."

At first the accident was diagnosed as merely a sprained and bruised ankle, and treated with massage. Rivy was well enough to dine out.

" In the evening I dined with Mrs. Ivor Guest—a tremendous dinner party of about fifty people. I hobbled in on crutches. The party was composed chiefly of pals of ours. I sat next to Lady Castlereagh and Walter Guinness. After dinner there was a small dance, which, of course, I could not take part in. However, I had a good yarn with Mrs. Asquith, who is a capital lady and always most interesting. I wish very much you had met her when you were here. I told her that I intended going to see her with you, and she told me she had been ill for the last ten months. She got on to the Education question, which was rather Greek to me, and I could only reply 'Yes' and 'No.' "

The ankle did not get better in spite of the most drastic massage, and when Rivy got on a pony he found that he could put no weight at all on his left stirrup. It kept him awake at night, and since his doctor told him to jump on it and use it as much as possible, he suffered a good deal of agony during the day. Nevertheless he went down to Hatfield for Whitsuntide, going up to London daily for treatment. On the Tuesday after Whitsuntide he came up to play in the Champion Cup at Hurlingham.

"I was unable to put a boot on, and so played in a large shooting boot and puttee. I also had my stirrup all padded up. In the first five minutes Ted Miller caught me an awful bump on the ankle, soon followed by another from George Miller. However, I stood it all right that ten, and played pretty well, considering that I could not hit the ball at all on the near side. I got one fairly good goal, having gone half-way down the ground. I thought that my leg would get better as I warmed up. However, this was not the case. The second ten I again played pretty well, but found it difficult to stop the ponies, as my grip was getting weaker. The third ten the pain began to be awful, and every bump that I got seemed to be on my bad ankle. By the fourth ten it felt rather like pulp, and to keep on at all I had to catch hold of the breastplate. We were having a tremendous match. At half-time the scores were 3—2. Gill, Jenner, and Roxburghe were playing like trumps. The Millers were a little off, and kept giving us openings; but I felt myself getting weaker and weaker, and could never turn my ponies in time to make use of them. The fourth ten we bombarded their goal, but in the fifth and sixth ten I was an absolute passenger and did not hit the ball at all. My ankle hurt fearfully. . . . I never was so glad of anything as when that game ended, and limped back very sore to the pavilion, where I had a very hot bath."

He went down to Hatfield that evening and got no sleep. Two days later he returned to London to have his ankle X-rayed. "Now comes the Waterloo part, for I found that instead of a sprained ankle I had a sprain on the outside and had broken the ankle bone on the inside. No wonder that I went through such pain. I went straight to Fripp, who told me that all the previous treatment had been entirely wrong. The worst thing I could do, of course, was twisting the ankle round, as the two bones were grating against each other. It seems a dream to me that I could have played in the Champion Cup with a broken ankle. Every time that any one bumped me in the polo match they were pushing these broken bones apart. No wonder towards the end of the match I squirmed when I saw anybody about to bump me."

That was the end of the polo season for Rivy, and there was nothing for it but to sell his ponies.* The episode was properly commented on by Francis. "It sounds a terrible experience, but I am glad *you* have been through it, as it shows *we* are made of the right stuff, though Heaven forbid me skipping on a bust ankle ! "

All that summer Francis was hard at work, for he proposed to take the qualifying examination for the Staff College, in order to gain experience. He was constantly deploring that he was so thick-headed about matters of military science, although his whole heart was in soldiering. On 26th July he writes :—

" Our drill this week has been the greatest fun in the world. Last Monday I commanded the squadron on a regimental

---

* He sold them most profitably. Mr. August Belmont, for example, bought "Cinderella" for £500.

parade—the first time in my life. It was rather a high trial, as, though we had been drilling slowly up to the present, the Colonel sounded the gallop at the start and drilled at the gallop for the rest of the day. I got on first-class. It is grand fun, as you are moving too quick to think, and if you make a mistake you cannot alter it. I was pleased, as I thought I knew no drill, but find I know a good deal more than many who have had a squadron some time."

He meditated much about the art of war in those days, and confided the results to Rivy, and he was perpetually harassed by the conviction that a fight with Germany was imminent. He used to plague his brother with questions about German politics and finance, and got but scrappy answers. One of his conclusions was that polo was an essential part of a soldier's education.

" I cannot understand why the infantry generals should be anxious to abolish polo—unless it be through ignorance. Has polo stopped John Vaughan, De Lisle, Haig, Hubert Gough, or any keen soldier ? "

Rivy had told him that Hugh Cecil's view was that it was more important for a country to have a good financial position than to have a good army when war broke out. This view Francis elaborately controverted, and was rather nonplussed to find that his uncle shared it.

He took the Staff College qualifying examination in the first week of August, and was very pleased with himself. The papers were far easier than he expected, and he thought hopefully of his future chances. As it turned out, it would have been impossible for him to qualify unless he bettered his languages, and it was this fact which made him so eager to spend his next leave in Germany. Immediately afterwards he started for manœuvres in the country north of Pretoria, along the Pietersburg line. He enjoyed himself immensely, and was especially proud of his hard physical condition.

" I find I stick hardships and discomforts far better than most. I have found my way about in this country by day and by night—no easy matter. I can outstay most of the others as regards fatigue. I seem to have got great confidence—far more than before—and I look on myself as as good a player as anybody else. Several chaps whom I used to look on as good I now look on as very bad."

His keenness was so great that in every letter he enlarged upon the danger from Germany.

" I think every serious person out here is awakened by Herr Dernburg's visit to this country. He is the Joe Chamberlain of Germany. I believe that the Dutch luckily hate the Germans, and will always support us against them."

Early in October Francis thought that he deserved a rest, and went on a short visit to Johannesburg.

" I wrote and asked a charming French *chanteuse* to come to lunch. She is the leading lady at the ' Empire,' at £200 a month. They are extraordinary, those French women. We were, besides her, five men, two of whom could not understand a word of French. She kept the whole table in fits of laughter, talking French all the time. I never met any one who said such things as she did. She fairly cleared the Carlton. Luckily, no one knew us. . . . In the evening we went to a dance at the County Club. You never saw such people—the *élite* of Jo'burg. The French lady turned up, much to the disgust of the Jo'burg society. She arrived very late, and only stayed half an hour. In that time she cleared out the room all right."

The autumn witnessed the annexation of Bosnia and Herzegovina by Austria, and Francis thought he saw a chance of a European war. He cabled to Rivy begging him to arrange with Harry Lawson to have him sent to Bulgaria as the correspondent of the *Daily Telegraph*. His brother John arrived in South Africa early in October, and Francis accompanied him on a visit to the Messina Mine. Most of his letters at this period are filled with uncommon good sense on the subject of the mine. He was convinced of its value, and anxious that his brother should give up all his time to it instead of going home to hunt. " Up here John seems to be lord of all he surveys, and yet he won't survey it."

The visit to Messina thoroughly unsettled him, and he found it hard to return to his books. " I am afraid you and I are very stupid," he wrote to Rivy. " I do not seem to get on at all like others seem to at these books, and I work three times as hard." He was inclined to be captious about his brother's attainments. " Not a very good letter from you this time. You are relapsing into your old tricks. I don't know how you discuss good and bad French when you don't know French at all. I am not quite clear what you are learning. Is it the French language or French literature ? The language, of course, is most useful, but I honestly think French literature is a waste of time to you. You know very little history, no geography—both subjects which arouse interests, form characters, and are essential for everyday life in London, and also for politics." Early in November he wrote : " I am determined, R. G., to take my work a little easier in future, and then work like fury for the 1910 August examination, and then take a year's holiday. Go a real bust— buy the best horse available, so as to win the National and Grand Military. Play polo seriously in 1911, and then go up for the exam. again the following year. So make a bit of cash, R. G., as my National horse will cost £2,000." But R. G. did not make a bit of cash that year. He lost the better part of £5,000 on their joint account, though he got most of it back later.

Francis paid a short visit in the early winter to the Duke of Westminster's estate in the Orange

River Colony, and then was seriously occupied with polo at Potchefstroom. At Christmas he had his usual solemn thoughts, which in this case dealt with love and the conduct of life.

" I think in marriage no half-way contracts ever are successful. You should either be damnably in love, so that there can be no doubt, or not propose at all. I expect our name is down against some lady whom we are to marry. . . . Some are married with the same speed that John tried to rush the Government out here. They then spend their lives wishing they had been refused. Every one wants a pal. I strongly recommend you to make greater pals with the Uncle. Try to live with him ; his company will improve your character, if you try to copy him, in every way. No man has more successfully worked in with other people, or gained more, by his generosity and *bonhomie*. Don't bury yourself with a book, or you become inhuman, despondent, and narrow. Mix your books with the Uncle and become a cheery, cultivated English gentleman."

But Rivy scarcely needed the advice, for he had not been troubling his books very much that year. He records that he tried in vain to read *David Copperfield*, always getting drowsy over it, so that he did not know whether it put him to sleep or he read it in his sleep. After his accident he became more or less of a butterfly, and his letters deal chiefly with country-house parties.

" Monday night I dined with Lady Alice Shaw-Stewart—a capital dinner party. I sat next to Lady Manners, and on her other side was Lord Cromer, and he talked most of the time to Lady Manners and me. He seemed a dear old boy. He has just gone on the committee of the Vivisection and Research League, and showed us a letter he had received from some woman, which abused him for about two pages and ended up, ' I had always looked on you as one of our greatest dictators, but now I see you are nothing but an inhuman brute.' Lady Manners asked him if he received many letters of this sort, and he said that in Egypt he got letters all the time saying that he was to be murdered next morning ; and then he added in a kind of undertone, ' Such damned rot, isn't it ? ' Last week he went down to stay near Winchester. The party consisted of Lord and Lady Cromer, Lord Elcho, and Lord Curzon. They went over to see Winchester on Sunday, when Lord Cromer overheard this from a Winchester boy, pointing at his party : ' There are some regular 'Arries and 'Arriets come nosing round here on a Sunday.' . . . I told him the story about Windham when Teddy Wood did his Latin prose and he failed. It made Lord Cromer roar with laughter. Lady Manners asked him if Windham was very clever. ' Well,' said he, ' he throws an extremely good salmon fly '—which I thought was rather characteristic.''

Rivy's letters were full, too, of politics. He discussed France with Miss Muriel White, and learned to his horror that that country was " honeycombed with republicanism." Apparently he was not aware of the nature of the French constitution. He met the McKennas at Nuneham, and considered the then First Lord of the Admiralty a " capital chap of the hail and hearty sort." He had frequent talks with Mrs. Asquith—" a magnificent lady, as you never have to say a word." From Mr. Asquith he heard something which confirmed his growing unfavourable opinion of the City. "He told me that in talking with financiers and asking their opinion he always found that they based their argument on no foundation—in fact, had no logic. I think this is very true. There is a famous Jew who, when asked about his partner's capacity for making money, said he had a wonderful *nose* for it. I think that is the only way to put it." He spent a week with Lord Ridley at Blagdon, Northumberland, assisting him to defend a case in the police courts, where he was accused of furious driving. "Mat is a landlord of the right old English sort —works very hard, and has the right notion of helping everybody." On that occasion he was taken to see the Roman Wall, of which he then heard for the first time.

In August he went with a company of the Scots Greys on manœuvres, and had the time of his life. They were very celebrated manœuvres, and led to furious disputes in military circles. Rivy was present at all the pow-wows, and recorded them with such gusto for the benefit of Francis that that exile was moved to remark, "It is an extraordinary thing, but the only two chaps who seem to enjoy manœuvres are F. G. and R. G. the banker." But the manœuvre letters contain other things than the tactics of General Scobell.

" On Thursday I dined with Cis Bingham at
the Brigade Headquarters. Molly Crichton and
Muriel Herbert came over from Wilton ; the
Duchess of Westminster, who was staying in a
village two miles off, was to have come but didn't.
We had some capital chaff. Afterwards Hugh
Grosvenor and I mounted horses and went across
the Plain to draw the Duchess. We nearly got
lost, but ultimately found her house. She had
gone to bed (Lady Shaftesbury was staying there
also), so we yelled at her window till finally the
owner of the house, an old farmer, let us in. We
soon had her down in a glorious silk dressing-
gown, and made her dig out some supper for us.
I did not get back until about 1 a.m. . . . On
Friday afternoon I hacked over to tea with Malise
Graham, and dined with the 1st Life Guards.
After dinner we suddenly heard a band approaching—could not think what it was, so went outside,
when it sounded ' Charge,' and about sixty fellows
from the 1st Brigade fell on the old Households,
and we had a desperate conflict. I kept out as
much as I could. Brother John was dining with
the 21st, so he accompanied them. Suddenly
some one called out, ' It's that Rivy !' and fell
on *him*, at which about four fellows sat on his
head. I returned to my camp about 11, to
find Allenby's Brigade were attacking Fanshawe's.

They broke everything in the Greys' and Bays' tents. It amused me awfully; but how young those fellows are to like a sort of ' rouge scrimmage ' still ! "

In the autumn Rivy's mind turned to more serious matters, and he took to himself a French tutor. Francis had advised him to spend his week-ends in Oxford and study there ; but he found that impossible. Rivy's letters about this time are little more than a medley of City gossip, mingled with notes of his engagements. On the Eton Memorial he wrote : " I do not think it necessary for us to spend more money on this. I sent this summer six boys and two girls from the Eton Mission to Juanita's cottage for a fortnight each. I think this is a much better way of spending one's money than by subscribing to bricks and mortar for rich Eton boys *not* to go into." He went to Hatfield, where he made friends with the present Lord Spencer; to the play with David Beatty, and discussed war in the East ; to a dinner where Sir Hugh Bell instructed him in economics ; and occasionally to the House of Commons. He went shooting with Mr. Pierpont Morgan. " Jack made me laugh very much. The Old Berkeley comes to his place twice a year. He made a remark to me which I thought would amuse you : ' I do not mind boarding two or three foxes for them, but ten's too many.' " In December at North Mimms he met Mr. Spender of the *Westminster Gazette* and Lord Harcourt, and heard much political talk. " X. was sure that Lloyd George was a Protectionist and would one day be found on the Protectionist side. If the Liberal Government were defeated at the next election, the Tories would bring in Tariff Reform at once ; this would split both parties, and new parties would be formed. Probably Lloyd George, and possibly Winston, would take the attitude that they had fought for Free Trade, but that, now the country had accepted Protection, unwillingly they must follow and form a Protection Radical Party. The Government most certainly would not go out this winter, but might after the Budget." So much for the prophets !

The year 1909 was for Francis a period of intense activity, both of body and mind. He was in exuberant health, and something in the diamond air of South Africa so enlarged his vitality that in everything he undertook he rejoiced " as a young man about to run a race." He began on the first day of the new year by winning the lemon-cutting prize at the South African Military Tournament. " Every one was very surprised, as honestly I had never tried it before. I never dreamed

I could cut a lemon, but I proved to be the only one who could cut both twice." He nearly won the tent-pegging too, and got into the final of the jumping. " I wish," he laments, " Staff College work came as easy as sports." That week he made the acquaintance of Lady Selborne. " I never liked a lady more. She is Linkie [Lord Hugh Cecil] in a comic mood in petticoats." He returned to Potchefstroom, but found his study much interfered with by the conditions of life there, so at the end of January he went back to Johannesburg, hired a room, and sat down to his books. " Here I have read from 6 to 8.30 geography ; 10 to 1, the *Times* and organization ; 2.45 to 4.15 I have done French lessons ; 4.30 to 7, mathematics ; dinner 7.15 ; then I read till about 10. You cannot imagine what a difference it makes to my work to work undisturbed. At Potch. I never sit down without being interrupted." In February he was back at Potchefstroom, where he now took a room in the town. This was his programme : " About 10.30 I drive at full speed to my room and work till 2.15. I gallop back to a late lunch at 2.30 ; then practise or play polo. Commence work again at 5 in the town, and do not move till 9 ; then home, small supper, read a little, and go to bed. I thus, in addition to polo and three hours riding, do eight hours' work. Every one thinks I am mad, but I know I am all right. Four hours at a sitting make the whole difference."

Francis's letters are full of the results of his new studiousness. For one thing he had come round to a belief in novels as an adjunct to the study of history.

" Few stolid history books tell you where Napoleon was wounded, or how Lannes died, or how Napoleon gained information of the Austrian position. Nor do they tell you that one of the chief causes of the failure of Massena in Spain was because he had Mlle. X. with him. He failed to pursue Wellington because Mlle. X. was tired. Ney refused to obey his orders since they had quarrelled because Ney found himself sitting next Mlle. X. at dinner. Junot quarrelled with Massena because his wife, a princess, refused to speak to Mlle. X. or to stay under the same roof. Such information is gained from novels—in conjunction with history."

Sometimes there is military criticism :—

" I am thinking of writing to Colonel Repington to wake up our army about the use of machine guns. The nation which first studies them and employs them scientifically in the next war will gain an immense advantage over a nation which neglects their use. At present, I fear, we will be in the same position as the Austrians in 1866."

From March onward, plans for 1910 and 1911 began to be Francis's chief solace in his arduous labours. He implored Rivy not to sell his ponies, for in 1911 he meant to play polo hard, as well as ride in the Grand National. In March he was again in Johannesburg, recovering from a slight attack of fever, where he solaced his convalescence with Queen Victoria's *Letters*, dined with the Selbornes, and had lengthy talks with Mr. Walter Long about army reform. " I prayed him never to forget that an army without discipline was worth nothing. The American army had drilled in drill halls, wore fine uniforms, could shoulder a musket ; they also knew all the theory of marching. In practice they failed to march five miles, because streams, blackberry bushes, and tight boots took more hold of them than discipline and instinctive obedience, which is not obtained in a few hours' training." He was enthusiastic about the Union of South Africa, then in process of formation. " I am bound to say, R. G., that though we damned the Radicals for giving back this country, it seems to have been most beneficial. Of course things have turned out far better than they had any right to expect, but the result is the great thing."

For the next month his letters are more full of polo than of his studies. " I school my ponies every afternoon *myself*. It has made a surprising difference. My thoroughbred Argentine is very handy, kind, and speedy. Two months ago she was unmanageable, so I have ridden her two hours in the ranks every morning when there was no parade. She does two hours' steady trotting early, and at 11 she goes to the riding school for one hour. Every afternoon I school her or play her. The great mass of work at first had no effect, but by continuing it I wore her down, and now she is like a dog, so quiet and so kind." His future plans were sorting themselves out. He saw before him a chance of qualifying for the Staff College, but he was aware that he could not enter it until he improved in his languages ; so a long spell on the Continent in 1911 or 1912 was decided upon. But before that there was to be a sporting *annus mirabilis*. " You will be kept pretty busy when F. G. comes home. I intend having the best stud of ponies ; six hunters at Melton ; the smartest charger that will win at Olympia, and a GRAND NATIONAL WINNER and a TUTOR. We will kick off in September 1910."

In April the 9th Lancers won the South African Polo Championship, beating the 3rd Hussars by eighteen goals to *nil* (of which eighteen Francis scored twelve), and the 4th Hussars by nine goals to three. To celebrate the result Francis took a few days off in Johannesburg, staying with Hugh Wyndham. In April he had a fortnight's machine-gun course at Bloemfontein, and was suddenly struck with the diversity of his accomplishments. " It often amuses me when I sum up the number of things an officer is supposed to know. Yet every civilian says he does nothing. Here am I working at ten subjects for Staff College, and supposed to be (and believe I am) an expert at riding. I am qualified for the Intelligence Department, having done a month's course ; know my regimental duties ; and am now going very technically into machine guns ; in addition to being a qualified veterinary and engineering instructor. Yet this is only about a quarter of what most chaps can do."

In May he suddenly grew sleepless, and for a week or two was worried about his health. He finally cured himself by drinking hot milk before going to bed. Towards the end of the month he was busy with squadron training, and was inspected by Lord Methuen. " Providence smiled on us, and everything went off so well that the General almost fell off his horse with joy. His address at the end was as follows : ' I congratulate the squadron leader on the way you have drilled and fought to-day. I think it is the best squadron I have ever seen in my life.' I never saw a chap so pleased." He proposed to take his examination in August, and then in September either to go on a big-game expedition or to visit Madagascar to learn French. The second alternative was soon dismissed, for he discovered that it would take as long to get to Madagascar as to get to England ; but he did his best to persuade Rivy to join him in the big-game hunt. In June he was elected Secretary of the South African Polo Association, and at a polo dinner made one of his infrequent public speeches. " Every one said it was good. It was certainly a great deal the longest." He was very pleased, too, with the result of the Brigade parades, where he was congratulated by the inspecting General. " The Colonel showed me my confidential report. It seemed rather flattering : ' This officer is a candidate for the Staff College, and should make an excellent Staff officer (What Ho !). His most notable qualities are his excessive keenness and capacity for working ; a very good officer, a fine horseman, and a most thorough sportsman ' (! !)."

There was certainly no doubt about the excessive keenness of this very good officer. In the same letter he informed Rivy that in 1911 he intended to compete in the following events :—

1. Army Point-to-Point.
2. Grand Military.
3. Grand National.
4. Champion Polo Cup.
5. Inter-Regimental Cup.
6. Staff College.

" It would, of course, be a record to win the lot,"
he adds modestly ; " still, I hope to. I have
written to Marcus Beresford (talk to him at the
Turf, if you see him) and asked him for the best
trainer." A little later he sketches the following
brilliant programme :—

> " *Tableau.*
> " 1911.—F. G. winning Grand Military, Grand National,
> High Jump at Olympia, Champion Cup, Inter-Regimental,
> Army P.-to-P., Staff Nomination for having beaten all previous
> records! Cheers from R. G. in the stands! Cheers from
> Bonbright, who seizes the stakes !
> " I mean to have the best polo team and to improve polo,
> and if possible play for England and challenge the Yanks. I
> mean to have two shots at the Grand National and Gold
> Cup. I mean to get into the Staff College. I mean to wake
> myself up and remember Sir Richard Grenville's dying words
> when his one ship took on fifty-four Spaniards, ' Fight on—
> fight on ! ' "

These ambitions did not interfere with his
laborious habits. On 1st August he notes that he
had done over ten hours a day for six weeks !
Then came the examination. " The flag dropped
on Wednesday," he wrote to Rivy, " since when
I have been up and over. I think I am still
going round, lying about third. We have a big,
broad fence on strategy, six hours' writing, and
then a nasty strong one in geography and French."
On the 16th he wrote : " It has been a great experience to me. It is a hard examination, and

requires numerous qualities to be successful. I got a little stale about the middle. I jumped some fences too big, others too low, and consequently pecked a good deal. I never came right off, and finished the course anxious to start again." The result was that in his papers Francis did well enough to qualify for the Staff College. It was a remarkable performance, for he did it entirely to gain experience, since he was not actually competing that year; and to undergo so drastic a discipline merely for training argued a real power of self-command.

For Rivy the first half of 1909 was clouded by misfortunes. His Christmas visit to Eaton had fallen through, and he spent the last week of 1908 alone in London, reading Queen Victoria's *Letters* and Gladstone's *Life*. He was glad of the solitude, for he had been rather depressed of late, reflecting upon the number of ragged ends in his life. " Still, I think if one *plugs*," so he consoled himself, " the horizon suddenly clears and you find you have ' arrived ' quite unconsciously. It is like polo : one plays (one thinks) badly against Buckmaster, but then go against a weaker team and you find you are in a class by yourself. When you feel downhearted, think of Lord Beaconsfield. He stood for Wycombe four times between the ages of twenty-eight and thirty-four, and was beaten each time by an enormous majority. At last he got in somewhere ; then made his first speech in the House, and every one roared at him, he made such a mess of it. But he didn't care a hang."

The depression was presently explained. Early in January he was threatened with appendicitis, but seemed to recover. He went down to stay with his uncle, Lord Grenfell, at Butler's Court, where his reading combined the *Life of Jack Sheppard* with the *Life of Queen Victoria*. " He was a notorious criminal of the eighteenth century, who did about twenty-four murders, and escaped from the condemned cell on four occasions. I described some of the details to Aline [Lady Grenfell], who hates horrors ; so the Uncle goes into the next room and takes out an old scrap-book in which there was a picture of him in 1876 superintending the execution of three niggers in Kaffirland, which nearly made Aline sick." Next week-end he went to Lillieshall, to the Duchess of Sutherland, where there was a cheerful party, and on the following Monday met Lord Haldane at dinner and discussed with him the Battle of Jena and the character of the Kaiser. " Haldane seems to me a wonderful cove." On the Wednesday, while at dinner, he suddenly got ill ; the doctors pronounced it acute appendicitis, and he was carried off to a nursing home. He was operated on at nine in the morning of 6th February by Sir Alfred Fripp. Not having acquired the operations habit, he took the matter very seriously, made a new will leaving everything to Francis, and composed a letter to his brother, only to be sent if he should not recover. In that letter he wrote :—

" I do not mind the idea of the thing at all. I feel that even if it goes wrong it cannot be helped. I have had a mighty good life, and have left nothing behind to be ashamed of, and can face the next world with a clear conscience. . . . Work hard at your books. You have a good reputation in the army, and only books and seeing plenty of the world can get you on ; so whenever you feel lazy think that R. G. would like you to be working. Best love, F. G. You have been a good friend to me."

The operation was successful, and Rivy, though he had an uncomfortable fortnight, was intensely interested in his sensations.

" I can remember talking a great deal of rot for the next hour, and having a long discussion with the nurse as to what sort of cable should be sent you. She was awfully amused. I knew I was talking rot, and yet I could not help it. I said such things as this : ' Please cable to my brother at once that I have done the operation, and that I found it rather difficult to jab the appendix out, but that it was all done successfully.' I said I particularly wanted to see Angus McDonnell, but that if he came up they must show him on to the roof. This went on till about one, when I got more sane and more uncomfortable. . . . I have been very surprised at the way they feed you up. I have something every two hours, and since Tuesday have been on solid food and having brandy three times a day. It is on occasions like this that being a teetotaller pays. I am quite sure the brandy benefits me three times as much as it would the ordinary invalid."

Rivy's convalescence was slow, and horses were out of the question for a month or two. He spent a good deal of his time at Cliveden with Waldorf Astor, and at the end of March was back at business. About this time he wrote to Francis :—

"You say you are getting unsociable. I don't think this matters a hang. In fact, it is a good thing to want to be alone— it shows you have other interests ; but then you must counter-act this by making yourself pleasant when you happen to be with your brother officers, and live up or down to the person you happen to be with. You used to curse me for liking to be alone ; yet I never seem to be alone. How much better it is to be talking to Rose or Marbot about Napoleon than to X. about a girl in Jo'burg. You and I always tend to be too much in Society. In fact, we are thick-headed because we never have been alone, and so never read the ordinary books that most boys know by heart."

By a diligent régime and much dumb-bell exercise Rivy hoped to be able to play polo in May. Meantime he was much perturbed by Francis's wild schemes for 1911, for Francis, in almost every letter, urged the wholesale purchase of ponies. "You forget that to have fifty ponies you will want £20,000 a year. Unfortunately, some of us have a way of spending about three

times as much as we have, and so it becomes
necessary now and again to sell a pony. You
write very foolish remarks about ' you City chaps
always wanting to sell ponies.' If a mug happens
to bid me £300 for 'Sweetbriar' I shall certainly
sell her." Early in April he had a touch of influ-
enza, and his letters show it. "I have bought you
the Empire typewriter that you asked for. Miss
Friston says that it will take you some time probably to learn how to work it at any speed, but I
say it will take you an eternity. I would suggest
your writing some of your letters to your friends
(except me) by it. I cannot think what you have
bought it for, as the time you will be spending
learning this you might have spent in learning
how to outwit Wilhelm in the next Anglo-German
war." Again : "You always laugh at me over
money, but it is time you realized that I only
save because I know far more about it than you. . . .
You have about £16,000 in the world, and get on
it about £1,000 a year. How can you buy National horses, hunters, and the best polo ponies
on that ? You will, by spending more capital on
horses, have less to invest, and so will have far
less income. The only soldiers who ride steeple-
chases now are people like McCalmont, who has
about a million, and George Paynter, who has
£10,000 a year. These are facts, and cannot be

got away from ; so be content to be the best polo player in the best regiment, not a sort of mug steeplechase rider whom no one hears of, and who goes bust." In letter after letter Rivy laboured to win Francis from his grandiose schemes and confine his ambitions to polo. He wanted to make up a first-class team in which he should play No. 1 and Francis No. 2 ; but Francis was obdurate. " I am going for the National," he wrote, " the Grand Military, the Army P.-to-P., and our own Regimental cups. I will not hunt."

In May came the famous 1909 Budget, on which Rivy's comments show commendable moderation. " They have hit the rich from every corner, and so every one is crying out. Personally I think there is a great deal to be said in favour of these socialistic Budgets. Old Rothschild will not eat any less *foie gras* because he has to pay a little more for his motor cars." But books and politics and everything else were presently submerged by the challenge of the American team. For the rest of the summer Rivy's letters contained little besides polo, and even the student at Potchefstroom was stirred to enthusiasm. Rivy was tried for the English team, but did not ultimately get a place in it, for the committee thought that his operation had left him too weak. He accepted the decision loyally, and constituted himself the

whole-hearted champion of the team ultimately
chosen. The Americans greatly impressed him.
" They have taken the place by storm. Money is
absolutely no object at all. They have twenty-
five ponies—all English except one, and all costing
about £500 each. Instead of being bad players,
as everybody expected, they are remarkably good,
and their ponies are really wonderful. They not
only have their own, but all the ponies that other
millionaires have been buying during the last three
years."

In May he went for a week to Holland with
Lord Grenfell and his sister-in-law. " He and I
went out one morning early, and were looking at
some rather nice biblical pictures in a shop window when we suddenly heard a terrific squealing.
' By Jove,' said the Uncle, ' they are killing a pig.'
So off we went at top speed, to find some wretched
pigs not being killed, as he had hoped, but being
dragged from a high cart and being weighed for
market. ' Most instructive,' said the Uncle. ' I
should never have known how to catch a pig.'
We went also to a diamond-cutting place, and saw
where the Cullinan diamond was cut. It was
difficult to get into, so I made the Uncle tell the
Jew boy at the door that he was ' Gold Stick in
Waiting ' to the King. You never saw such a
wonderful effect as it had on the nosy brigade.

They showed us a cup given by the King, on which were inscribed the words : ' To Benjamin, Joseph, and Moses Asscher, for services to the King of England '—which amused us very much indeed."

After that there is nothing but polo. Rivy records how at one match he heard a lady in a stand saying, " Why do we not breed such ponies as that in this country ? The Americans understand everything so much better than we do." " Whose was the pony ? None but the famous ' Cinderella,' sold by R. G. to the Americans at the end of last year. There is a good deal of rot like this being talked." Rivy played very well in some of the trial matches, and for long it was a nice question whether he would not be chosen for England. He watched the performances of his old " Cinderella " with intense interest. " They play her in plain double bridle, but she does not seem quite so handy as when I had her. She has her near fore all wrapped up in cotton wool. I would laugh if she broke down, for, as a Jew once said, ' Ze Christians have ze shares and ve ze cash '—the Yankees have the pony and I the cash, with which I bought two others."

His letters about this time are so technical that they scarcely bear reprinting, but they seem to me to contain the complete philosophy of polo, and I have no doubt that Francis greatly benefited by them. Rivy had made up his mind that if the cup were lost he and Francis would make up a team which would recover it, and he studied every detail of every game, and especially the American method of pony management, with an acumen which might have made his fortune on the Stock Exchange. When the disastrous final match was played and the cup was lost, Francis wrote :—

" A very good letter from you full of how we are going to beat the Yanks, but a telegram has appeared announcing England's defeat by 18 to 7. . . . I await your explanations. We must now put our backs to it and go to America and get the cup back. It will give us a dashed good goal to work up for, and all England will give us a cheer. We must lie doggo for two or three years and practise, practise, practise. Will you take it on ? I have never really laid myself out for polo as I am going to do now. Every yokel here is discussing our defeat. I don't suppose in any colony there is a European who has not heard of it. So up, ye men, and at 'em ! "

Rivy's comments on the final match seem to me very sound. " The American ponies are undoubtedly better than ours : they jump off quicker and go in quicker. As for the striking of the Americans, they hit the polo ball as if it were a racquet ball. They are truly wonderful. Whenever they get away they get a goal. This, as you know, is exceedingly rare on English ground.

Freake and Pat Nickalls, whom I have always admired as fine hitters, are children compared with the Yankees. The extraordinary part is that ' Cinderella' has proved by far the best pony on the American side. I do not know what they have done with her, or whether the English ponies are worse than they were last year, but on all sides yesterday I kept hearing, ' What a wonderful pony that is that Grenfell sold ! ' All the papers seem to rub it in, and it seems funny to think that this pony was hawking round London last year for six weeks and advertised in the papers before the Yankees bought it. I am now perpetually asked, ' Why on earth did you sell her ? ' My only answer is, ' Why on earth did I break my leg ? ' " He was very rightly furious at the attacks in the papers on the English team, especially before the final—" I thought it very unsportsmanlike of a decent paper to cut off the heads of the English players before they had gone on the field,"—and he wrote an excellent letter in the *Times* on this point. He summed up the situation thus to Francis :—

" Whitney determined to try to win this cup four years ago. For four years he has been collecting all the ponies he could, and all his team has been trained to play together. The Waterburys are two magnificent players. Larry is the champion racquet player of America. They have played polo since they were ten, and always together. To get the cup back we must do likewise."

Among the many entertainments given to the American team was a luncheon at the Pilgrims' Club, with Lord Grenfell in the chair. In the course of his speech he expounded the habits of his nephews. " I do not know if there is anybody present who is an uncle. If so I hope he has not been blessed with such nephews as the two that I have. One of them sits there ; the other, thank Heaven, is engaged in South Africa. I have a small estate in the country where I hoped to feed and fatten some cattle and sheep. On my return from abroad I found some very thin cattle, some thinner sheep, and some extremely fat polo ponies. On making inquiries, my bailiff told me that he had received instructions that these ponies (sent down without my permission) were to be kept ' in the field where the Uncle grows his hay.' The result was that I had no grass ; all the bark was torn from my trees ; there was an enormous hole in my hayrick—which I think 'Cinderella' used as a bedroom ; and in addition one day 'Cinderella' got loose and made a fine meal off my geraniums."

I think it may fairly be said that of all polo players in England Rivy was the first to divine the secret of the American success, and to begin, laboriously and scientifically, to lay plans to win back the cup. He was very clear that it was no use attempting the thing in 1910, and that England must lie low until she had trained a team adequate for the purpose. His own dream was that that team should consist of himself as No. 1, Francis No. 2, Hardress Lloyd back, and either Bertie Wilson or Noel Edwards as No. 3. He estimated that it would take £15,000 to collect ponies. " If you and I practise hard together," he wrote to Francis, " and discuss the thing every evening, we could, I am sure, become as good as the Waterburys. The whole American combination was due to them. They used to work out problems on the polo ground and then practise them. . . . It would be a big thing to do, and one worth *concentrating* on ; but if you are going to work for the Staff College and play this sort of polo, you must chuck all your other foolish ideas of steeplechasing."

On 28th July he went to America for his firm, and stayed on his arrival with Mr. Devereux Milburn. With his host and the Waterburys he went down to Newport to see a match for the American Champion Cup. He was much struck by the hardness and fastness of the grounds, which reminded him more of India than of England. His conclusion was that the average American player was not good, and that the Meadowbrook team who had won the cup in England were in a class by themselves. He spent some pleasant weeks in America, busy in his American office and occasionally spending a Sunday with Jack Morgan. On their joint birthday he wrote to Francis : " I hope this is the last birthday for some years that we shall be separated. Twenty-nine seems dashed old to me ; twenty-seven and twenty-eight always sounded young, but at twenty-nine we should start and be up and doing. I am getting on very well in my firm, and have really a great chance in the future. I made £1,500 this year, but, like an idiot, speculated last Christmas and lost some money and also spent about £2,000. Why do we spend such an infernal amount ? " He varied his business with reading a good deal of Shakespeare, and Bryce's *American Commonwealth*. One day he met an old Eton friend. " He amused me enormously, for he had, of course, got interested in a wonderful invention. Most people here are interested in large development schemes, but, just like a thin-headed Englishman, he has got a patent for closing whisky bottles. I did not like to suggest to him that the majority of people I met were searching for patents to open them."

About the middle of September he came back to England to dispose of a new business which his firm had acquired, where he found his groom in despair over Francis's African ponies, which had just arrived. " He wants to know what language they understand, as they don't seem to answer to English." At home he got the news of Francis's success in his examination. " I never was so surprised in my life as to find that you had qualified in everything. You must have become a sort of encyclopædia, for there was not one word in any paper that I could have answered. It seems astounding what one can learn by hard work, for I have always felt that you would never pass anything except possibly the entry exam. into Eton ! "

On 16th October he left again for America, and in the first week of November attended a dinner given to the American polo team. There he made a speech which was a huge success.

" These fellows have a pleasant way of suddenly calling upon you for a speech; so, as I was anxious to do it properly, I worked hard, not only at the words but at the delivery. At the dinner there were two hundred people collected from all parts of the U.S.A.—army officers from Wyoming, Canadian officers, Mr. Root (a member of the Cabinet), Mr. Bacon (Secretary of State), Mr. Milburn (head of the Bar), etc. I was not down to speak, and luckily the speeches were all very bad, with no jokes. I sat on the dais and was several times referred to, so that I felt I ought to say something. At the beginning of dinner I had told the chap next to me that Englishmen were very poor speakers. He said that it came quite natural to most Americans; so I said that nothing in the world scared me so much, and that I could not do it. Just before the end of the last speech I told him I felt I ought to say something, but did not know what to say. He thought it a capital joke, and sent a message to Whitney to call on me. I got up and, funnily enough, did not feel a bit nervous. It is an extraordinary feeling when you get hold of an audience. They roared at my jokes, much appreciated my references to Whitney and the way we admired him, and finally, when I sat down after fifteen minutes without a check, they all stood up and sang, ' For he's a jolly good fellow.' Mr. Root congratulated me, and Mr. Bacon said he had rarely heard a speech better delivered. I had to shake hands with everybody there. The Canadians were delighted that a Britisher should make a far better speech than any Yankee. My pal who sat next me told every one I had said I could not speak at all, and that I was quite unprepared. He thought me a sort of Demosthenes. Wasn't it luck? Francis Fitzgibbon was told on the Cotton Exchange next day ' that an Englishman had made the best speech that was ever heard of.' "

Altogether Rivy had a very pleasant time in America, getting through a great deal of business and making innumerable friends. Among his recreations he rated high the privilege of roaming through Mr. Pierpont Morgan's private library. " Some of the things simply took one's breath away, and I am surprised that the British Museum allowed them to get out of the country. He has all Macaulay's original letters and manuscripts, also Walpole's, Thackeray's, and Dickens's, etc., with scratchings out and alterations made with their own pens. Mr. Morgan, senior, is a jolly old boy with a very determined look. He has told me to go and see his library whenever I like."

Meantime Francis, having finished his labours,

thought of relaxation. He departed in the end of August for Barotseland in company with M. Chevally, the French Consul at Johannesburg. When they got into the lion country on the Kafue his companion grew restless. " I sleep in his tent. He got up three times in one night and asked my hunter if that was a lion, as he thought he heard a moan. Last night I said, ' It is so hot ; let us have the tent open.' ' All right,' he said, but the moment he thought I was asleep he got up and laced the tent down." M. Chevally, who had not come out to hunt, presently returned home, and Francis went northward into the thick bush of the Kafue region. His letters to Rivy are filled with the usual details of African hunting, and in deference to his brother's profession he intercalates observations on trade. " The few traders I have seen are remarkable for their lack of organization. I have met four. All are broke, and yet at times make £5,000 a year." He greatly admired his hunter, " an old filibuster who used to trade in poached ivory. He has had over £30,000 to his credit, but is now, like most, broke. He is a sort of Starlight in *Robbery under Arms*, and has twice been tried for murder. He began, as in novels, by being shipwrecked off Quilimane in 1869 or thereabouts, the Portuguese being then at war with the natives. A Jew in Quilimane supplied the natives with powder, which my chap carried through to them and was paid £1,000."

After leaving the Kafue Flats he rejoined the railway and went on to Broken Hill, whence he intended to trek towards Lake Nyassa. So far he had done fairly well with buck, having got eland, lechwe, roan, reedbuck, oribi, and wildebeest. At Broken Hill he was entertained by Charles Grey,* and had much trouble with his hunter, who was drunk for two days. " I have been in the most awful places after him. He broke into my chest and got rid of four bottles of brandy."

In the beginning of October he was on the Loangwa River. " Charming country, big rivers, high hills, good trees; but Providence (Whose doings we cannot understand) has provided a Tsetse Fly that worries you all day." There he got a charging rhino at about twenty yards, and had a stiff hunt after that most dangerous of quarries, the African buffalo. " I led the attack, cleared for action, with a nigger behind me to keep me on the spoor. We went through very high thick grass, like that stuff we got tiger out of in India. The niggers at first refused to go in. After seven hours' pursuit we passed a tree up which, luckily, we put a nigger, and so spied the

* Younger brother of Lord Grey of Fallodon.

buffalo lying down fifty yards ahead. I climbed the tree like a monkey and killed him. The whole hunt lasted eight hours : we started just before daylight on the spoor, and killed the buffalo at 1.30—walking all the time in the middle of a Central African summer." A little later he tried for an elephant, but had no luck, though he had four separate hunts, each taking about four days' hard walking. Presently he came to the conclusion that he had had enough of it. " It made my mouth water," wrote Rivy, " to hear that you were surrounded by about 6,000 big game, while I am surrounded by about 6,000 big noses of the Jewish fraternity." But hunting, as Francis found it, was too monotonous a pursuit to satisfy him indefinitely. " It is extraordinary what regular walking does. I look on fifteen miles as nothing. Last week I did twenty miles and shot a hippo after it before sundown. That means a walk from Wilton Park to Ascot." This is the young gentleman who in India had decided that Providence did not mean him to use his legs otherwise than on horseback ! On his journey down country he did 150 miles on foot in six and a half days. On the 8th of November he was back in Potchefstroom. " I am exceedingly glad I have done the trip, but somehow I do not feel very anxious to do it again. But it has been a most thorough mental rest."

The effects of the mental rest and the hard training which Francis had enjoyed were speedily apparent in his letters home. He discovered in himself a strong disinclination to turn his attention to books. His thoughts were all now on physical culture, on polo, and on his approaching return to England. He pled with Rivy to buy ponies, all of the best and as many as possible. " If you will not spend the money yourself, for Heaven's sake spend mine." He repudiated with scorn the suggestion that he should write of his Central African experiences in a magazine. " Don't you become a Jew boy," he told his brother, " because you live among them. I will never, never write to a magazine. Nothing does a soldier more harm. Every person has his own job, and the successful man is he who knows what is his and sticks to it. Literature and money-making are not mine, and I intend to interfere in neither. I think you are very ill-advised to be always looking for cheap advertisement." The great sporting events for which he intended to enter monopolized his mind. At a boxing match, observing that one of the combatants sipped champagne between rounds, he came to the conclusion that even a teetotaller like himself might benefit by a little dope before a big match, so he implored Rivy to get the best medical opinion on the subject. He was not prepared to abate one jot of his ambitions. "You will be miserable," he wrote in his Christmas letter, "to hear that I have definitely decided to try to win the National in 1911 and 1912. So my next few years will be busy to become (1) best polo player at No. 2 ; (2) to win the National ; (3) to become a p.s.c. Best love, old boy ; don't become too studious, or you will become too old too soon. . . . Please stop going to theatres until I arrive, as it is miserable to come home full of cheer to find a *blasé* brother whose method of entertainment is to give you a dinner at the Bath Club ! We are going to have none of that. We will kick off at the Ritz, and laugh at the Gaiety." In this mood of vaulting ambition and ecstatic vitality Francis's period of soldiering abroad reached its close.

CHAPTER VI.

1910–1914.

THE next four years saw the Twins together in England—Francis with his regiment at various stations, and Rivy immersed in City business, yet not so immersed that he could not spare time for partnership in many sports. It was a happy period, for neither had ever been quite at ease out of the other's sight. They had now passed their thirtieth year, and, so far as Providence would permit, had grown up. This maturity was not marked by any decline of the high spirits of youth, but by a growth in placidity and a modest contentment with life. Rivy, in especial, was now less of an anxious pilgrim, less habitually tormented by a desire for the moon. He seemed to be on the road to great business prosperity, for in January 1910 he joined his brother Arthur's firm, then at the height of its success ; his reputation in sport was solidly established, and he was inclined to acquiesce in that shrinking of horizons which is the tragedy of the transition from youth.

Francis, in whom ambition woke more spasmodically, had his hands full with his Staff College and regimental work, and his mind preoccupied with the endless interests of the returned traveller. Merely to be at home again was to him a perpetual wonder and delight.

I had known the Twins off and on for some years, but at this period we became intimate friends. London is a place of many casual acquaintances, much blurred in the memory, but I think that no one who was brought into contact with Francis and Rivy was likely to forget them. They had that complete detachment from the atmosphere which we call distinction. If it was not always easy to tell one from the other, it was impossible to confuse them with anybody else. Just over six feet in height, beautifully proportioned, and always in hard training, they were most satisfactory to behold. Once Rivy, hastening away from a ball, asked what he took to be the butler to call him a hansom. " Indeed, I call you handsome, my boy," said the " butler," who was Mr. Choate. Their clear, pale complexions, derived from a Spanish strain, their dark hair and eyes, and something soft and gracious in their manner gave them a slightly foreign air ; but their deep explosive voices were very English. Both had a trick of finishing a sentence with a

kind of gust of deep-breathed emphasis. The
predominant impression, I think, that they made
on the world was of a great gentleness and an
inexhaustible vitality. Neither could be angry
for long, and neither was capable of harshness
or rancour. Their endearing grace of manner
made a pleasant warmth in any society which they
entered ; and since this gentleness was joined to
a perpetual glow of enthusiasm the effect was
triumphant. One's recollection was of something
lithe, alert, eager, like a finely-bred greyhound.
Most people are apt to be two-dimensioned in
the remembrance even of their friends, like the
flat figures in a tapestry ; but Francis and Rivy
stood out with a startling vividness. Even death
has not made them sink into the background of
memory. When I think of either it is as of youth
incarnate, with all the colour and speed of life,
like some Greek runner straining at the start of
a race.

Francis arrived in January 1910, and was at
once laid hold of by politics. The Twins hunted
in couples through that unsavoury Budget election
when the spirit of Limehouse was abroad, and
spoke at many meetings, chiefly of railwaymen
and workmen. It is not recorded what Francis
said, though he can have known as much about
English politics as about the Ptolemaic system; but

he was reputed an effective canvasser, and it is on record that on one occasion he looked after a labourer's baby while the father went to vote, and afterwards had supper with the family. He went to the depot at Woolwich for some weeks, and then joined his regiment at Canterbury. He took great pains with his lectures to his men, and such specimens as I have read are admirable, both for their clear statement and for the enthusiasm with which he managed to invest his treatment. He was a slow worker, and took a long time to understand a thing, but once he had grasped it he could impart it vigorously to others. He laboured always to inspire in his hearers a passion for the 9th Lancers, dwelling on the great episodes of their past, and usually at the end compelling his audience to stand up and cheer for the regiment.

That summer was devoted to polo, and for the moment Francis's steeplechasing ambitions seem to have been at rest. The Old Etonian team in which the Twins played carried everything before it, and was invited by the Hurlingham Committee to go to America to try for the cup. They decided to be entirely independent of the America Cup Recovery Fund, which was to remain intact and provide the sinews of war for the great effort of the following year. That summer, I think, may be taken as the height of the Twins' fame in the polo world. It may not be out of place to quote some notes written by Lieutenant-Colonel E. D. Miller after their death.

" The polo world mourns many fine players and good sportsmen killed in the war, but for none is more sorrow and regret expressed than for the gallant Twins. I knew Rivy intimately for a considerable time before I met Francis. I think it was in 1902 that his older brother Cecil asked me to take him to Spring Hill and teach him the rudiments of polo. He came and spent a happy month, working like a stable lad and putting his whole heart and soul into his work.

" My first meeting with Francis was at Tattersall's a year or two later, when, mistaking him for Rivy, I warned him not to buy a good-looking pony that he was inspecting. It was typical of the Twins' liking to be mistaken for one another that he merely thanked me for my information, and did not divulge the fact that he was not Rivy, although he spent some time in my company looking at other ponies in the yard. Rivy was undoubtedly the better and stronger player of the pair, but when they were playing together it was extraordinarily difficult to tell them apart, their horsemanship and style being very similar. They were both brilliant players, and were much better when playing together than separately. They studied every detail of the game and took the most enormous trouble in the purchase and training of their ponies. They were great advocates for speed, and were the only players I knew who kept a trial pony and raced him against anything they were likely to purchase. They were as hard as iron, and always kept themselves very fit, and were (especially Rivy) very fine horsemen. Rivy used to ride the stronger and more difficult ponies. His pluck was phenomenal.

" Rivy played No. 1 with Francis No. 2, and their combination and tactics were more perfect and highly developed than any pair in England. Had they been spared they would probably now be chosen to represent their country in the next

International match. They modelled their play on that of the Waterbury brothers, and though they were not quite as brilliant performers as the Americans, their tactics and understanding were just as perfect. The Twins, as at everything else in life, played polo with one mind. Francis held a record in that he played in the winning team of the Champion Cup in England, India, Africa, and America. No one else has done this.

"Good players and fine sportsmen as they were in first-class polo, where they will be most missed will be on the social side, for they were always the life and soul of country-house polo tournaments. As a polo manager no one knew better than I did what a wonderful help they were in making a success of the kind of tournament that used to take place at Eaton and Madrid. They would always pull out and play on any side with any one, in order to make a success of the entertainment from the host's point of view, and neither of them cared two farthings if they won or lost so long as they could help the show and make every one happy. . . . The Twins have left behind them a reputation quite unsurpassed for pluck, clean living, unselfishness, and charm."

The Old Etonian team as originally fixed was made up of Francis and Rivy, Lord Rocksavage and Lord Wodehouse. Lord Wodehouse found himself unable to go, so on 6th August Francis and Rivy started with Lord Hugh Grosvenor— Lord Rocksavage and Mr. F. A. Gill being already in America. The Twins took for their reading the following odd assortment : *A Constitutional History of the United States*, *Life of Stonewall Jackson*, *Vanity Fair*, *Jorrocks*, *Pickwick Papers*, *Les Misérables*, a primer of geography, *The Life of Nelson*, and *The Confessions of a Princess*.

Francis had a bad arm when they left, and when they reached America it was found that he could not play. The side accordingly called itself Ranelagh, and was made up of Rivy, Mr. F. A. Gill, Lord Rocksavage, and Lord Hugh Grosvenor. Later Francis resumed his place, and they became once again the Old Etonians. The team had a brilliant career at Narragansett and in Canada, winning nearly every match they played, though, as they were not official challengers, they could not compete for the cup. It was essentially a trial trip, and the players learned a vast deal which was of value to later challengers. I find a paper of Rivy's in which he summarized the result of his experience, expounding in the most minute detail what he had learned in America on the transport and training of ponies. He went into everything, including the price of oats, but the most valuable lesson is contained in this passage :—

" In America the game, owing to the better grounds and the 'no off-side' rule, is very much faster than it is in England, and the pony requires to have his lungs quite clear. The player gets away much more often than at home. The game is not nearly such a rough-and-tumble one, and so players do not require such staying power as in England. What they require is to be able to go with these tremendous bursts. A pony should be trained to play its utmost speed. A point that we learned, which improved our play enormously in this somewhat scrambling game, was that instead of stopping a pony on its hocks after a run, it is far quicker to turn it on a circle. This does not tire the pony nearly so much, nor the rider, and by being able to pass the ball forward the player can often, even if unable to hold his pony properly, do a lot of work. At Newport my grey pony, owing to its being wrongly bitted, was quite out of hand; but by turning it on a circle and the others passing the ball to me, I played very well, and no one noticed that I did not have proper control." *

While Rivy was busy with polo Francis thought that he might employ his leisure in visiting the battlefields of Virginia. He went first to Bull Run and Manassas Junction. At Winchester he met Dr. Graham, a Presbyterian minister who had known Stonewall Jackson, and who told Francis many details of his hero. He then visited Kernstown, and at Richmond met Dr. Jeremy Smith, who had been Jackson's A.D.C. after Second Manassas, from whom he picked up much information about his singular kinsman, Colonel St. Leger Grenfell, who had served on the Confederate side in the war. He spent much time studying the field of Gaines Mill, and met the eponymous Mr. Gaines, who had been absent through a fever from the fight. He returned to Newport with a Confederate flag as a relic, and a

* England challenged America the following year (1911), when the team consisted of Hardress Lloyd, Noel Edwards, Bertie Wilson, and Leslie Cheape, the last three of whom fell in the Great War. It failed, after a most brilliant effort, to defeat the American team, which was composed of the Waterburys, Mr. Whitney, and Mr. Milburn. In 1914 a team organized by Lord Wimborne, composed of F. W. Barrett, Leslie Cheape, Vivian Lockett, and H. A. Tomkinson, recovered the cup for England.

Francis on "Michael" and Rivy on "Cinderella."

new appreciation of the great campaign and the great leader, who for years had filled the first place in his affections.

There is little to record for the rest of 1910. At Christmas the Twins went with a tutor to Brussels and made an elaborate study of the field of Waterloo. Throughout the early months of 1911 Francis was busy with his work for the Staff College, and embarked on authorship with a letter in the *Times* on the Sydney Street affair, in which he stoutly defended Mr. Churchill's action in employing soldiers and machine guns.

In April, on the invitation of King Alfonso, the two brothers went to Madrid to play polo. On their way they paid a visit to their favourite statue, that of Hercules and the Wild Boar in the Louvre, which Rivy had had copied as a memento of his Kadir Cup victory. They arrived at Madrid on 9th April, and stayed with the Duke of Alba, where Francis was so much impressed with the pictures and tapestry that his diary reads like an auction catalogue. Next day they left for Moratalla, the Marquis of Viana's house, where the polo party was assembled, which included the King, the Duke and Duchess of Santonia, the Marquis Villarieja, and the two Millers. That fortnight in Spain was one of the best holidays in the Twins'

experience. Francis records at length his con-
versations with the King, which covered every
subject from polo to high politics. " He told me
that one of the ambitions of his life was to play
with his regiment, the 16th Lancers, in the Inter-
Regimental. He would undertake to provide them
with the best ponies. He understood they were
going to India for eight years. By that time he
would be thirty-two and at his prime, and hoped
by then to be good enough. He had great difficulty in playing polo in England, as King Edward
said it was too dangerous ; so he thought it best
to ask nobody's advice, and just went and played
at Rugby. He could not understand why a king
should be brought up like a hothouse plant.
The only occasions on which he had been nearly
killed were (1) when he was driving in a carriage
where the horses were led by men on foot, and
(2) when driving very slowly in Paris. X. re-
marked that he had had a letter from the Crown
Prince of Germany to say he wanted to play polo
when he came over this summer. ' Good,' said
the King ; ' then that will make it easier for me
when I go over.' We suggested a match against
the Crown Prince ; at which he said, ' Ah yes, I
think I will win. The Germans are very slow.' "

The polo consisted of matches between the
King's side and Alba's side, Rivy playing with

the first and Francis with the second. The weather was abominable, and the Twins seem to have had more walking about in wet gardens than polo. On 13th April the party returned to Madrid, where Francis and Rivy stayed again with Alba, and found there the Duchess of Westminster and Lady Helen Grosvenor. That day being Maundy Thursday, they went to the Palace to see the function of the Lavatorio, when the King and Queen wash the feet of twelve beggars. Francis's diary contains a spirited description of this curious function, and pages and pages about the pictures in the Prado Museum, which impressed him more than anything else in Spain. In Madrid they played polo on the King's private ground, but the weather was unpropitious and the games poor. The King gave instructions that Francis should be shown all over the cavalry and infantry barracks, and when he expressed a desire to see the tapestries, ordered every one in the Palace to be specially hung up for him. Various bull fights and a short visit to Seville, where they saw part of the Easter Feria, brought to an end a trip which both regarded as one of the most crowded and delightful experiences of their lives.

In June Rivy attended the Coronation with his uncle's children, who were much excited to see the Field-Marshal in the procession. He wrote an account of it to Lady Grenfell, and, knowing her dislike of horrors, wickedly described at some length an hour he passed in the Scotland Yard Museum. " I wish you had been with us. I am sure you would have loved seeing the finger of a burglar that was pulled off as he tried to get over a gate and was caught up. It is preserved in spirits of wine." In July the King of Spain came to England and lunched at their brother Arthur's house at Roehampton, going with the Twins afterwards to a polo match.

That summer saw the Agadir crisis, and Francis naturally decided to be present at the French manœuvres. It does not appear that he ever received the permission of the French Staff, but a small thing of that kind was not likely to stop him. He attended the manœuvres of the VI. Corps in the Verdun area during September, living with the 6th Cuirassiers, and sent an excellent report to the War Office. He was much struck by the horses of the cavalry. " They are bought from three and a half years old and sent to the Remounts until four and a half. They are then sent to a regiment and trained for two years before being put into the ranks. This system of teaching the horse to carry the man is a great improvement on ours of teaching the man to ride a partly-trained horse." He thought that the cavalry did not realize the value of the rifle and had no notion of mounted infantry work. This was not unnatural in the case of the Cuirassiers, who, owing to their cuirasses, could not, of course, aim with a carbine. " I put on a cuirass myself and made certain of this," adds Francis. He was not greatly impressed by the system of reconnaissance. " The men returning from patrols deliver their messages very clearly, but invariably get the names of the villages mixed up, and it seems to me that by far the best, simplest, and quickest method of sending in reports is for each man to have a map and to mark on it all he sees." The French horsemastership he thought poor. " The saddles, weighing when loaded up about eight or nine stone, are never taken off. They are put on sometimes an hour before start-ing, and often left on an hour or so after the troops have got in. One night the cavalry division I was with marched at 10 p.m., halted from 2 a.m. to 6.30 a.m., during which time the horses were not fed or the girths even loosened, and the horses received no food or water until 3 o'clock the follow-ing afternoon." He thought, however, highly of the French infantry, and loved their habit of singing on the march. He was impressed by the mechanical-transport arrangements, and most pro-foundly by the use of airplanes. He went up—

his first attempt of the kind—in a Farman bi-plane, and became a whole-hearted convert to the value of air reconnaissance. Most of the officers he thought too old for their jobs. " Regimental commanders vary from fifty-five to sixty, squadron leaders from forty to fifty, and brigadiers from sixty onward."

These are quotations from his official report. His diary contains more interesting matter. He found that the French Army expected war, and awaited it with calm and confidence. Even if it did not come that year, they considered that it was certain to come within three years. He gives amusing descriptions of cavalry charging cavalry and pulling up facing each other. " Imagine two divisions charging in England, stopping head to head and no accident." He declares that he never saw a single horse out of hand. On the other hand, the cavalry seemed to him to have a passion for charging and little else—to know nothing about reconnaissance or dismounted action. " I spoke to a Staff officer, who said that the French would lose heavily in war. He gave as an instance a cavalry division passing in front of an infantry battalion in column of route, when it ought to have dismounted two squadrons and made a detour." Francis's general comments are, as usual, very shrewd. He saw that the danger of

the French Army was its passion for persistent
and often unconsidered offensives, and that it had
no adequate training in defensive warfare. An
almost mystical belief in the attack at all times
and in all circumstances was being preached in
the schools of war and practised on manœuvres.
For the rest, he received great kindness and made
many friends. Among these was General Joffre,
and on one occasion, being stranded far from his
quarters, he cadged a lift in a car from a gentleman who turned out to be M. Humbert.

In October we hear of Rivy staying at Glamis
Castle, where he laboured earnestly to discover
the celebrated mystery. " Old Beardy has so far
eluded us, but we are on his track. I found that
my room was next door to the Hangman's room,
where no one has slept for fifty years. Last night
when all was quiet, with the assistance of my next-
door neighbour, I moved my mattress and blankets
into the Hangman's, and slept there happily on
the floor till 6 a.m., when I woke up and found
my door ajar, though it was shut last night. We
may not have banged it enough, so we are going
to experiment again to-night. It is great fun
here ; all the ladies and some of the men are in
a blue funk." This is not quite the whole of
that story. Rivy woke at midnight to find the
door open, and to his consternation it refused to

close. He prepared his soul for horrors, when he discovered that the reason of the door's refractoriness was the presence of one of his slippers. After that he fell asleep, and awoke, as he says, at 6 a.m. to find the door again open.

Some time that year he became interested in the Invalid Children's Aid Association, and the following year became Treasurer and Chairman. He enabled Islington, St. Pancras, and Holloway to become a separate branch by guaranteeing expenses. Early in the morning before going to the City, or after a long day full of engagements, he would go and see some of the " cases " in their homes. Both the Twins kept up this interest to the end ; the Islington branch now bears their name ; and it is in aid of a memorial fund to carry on their work that this little memoir has been written.

After returning from the French manœuvres Francis went through a musketry course at Hythe, and presently took up racing on a modest scale. A bad fall in November in a steeplechase at Sandown gave him concussion, the effects of which lasted for nearly six months. At Christmas he was in bed, and early in the New Year he went to Dr. Crouch's open-air cure. Meantime, at the end of January, Rivy departed for Mexico on business. The great event of his trip was that he got mixed up in a battle about sixty miles from Mexico City, where the Zapatistas were giving trouble. It was a small affair, but it was his first experience under fire, and he wrote a lengthy account to Francis. The Twins liked to have all their experiences in common, and it had always been a regret to Rivy that Francis had been in action and he had not. " Everybody in this country appears to have a predisposition to let the enemy know their exact movements. The operations of the following day were discussed all Sunday in Cuernavaca, and I suppose the Zapatistas were told exactly what our general proposed to do—with the result that we went to the battle and the Zapatistas didn't."

Francis was far from well all summer, still suffering from the effects of his accident; so he went to Berlin in June, partly for the change and partly to learn the German language, without which he could not hope to qualify for the Staff College. He stayed with a retired German officer called Hamann, a friend of Mr. Austen Chamberlain, and a godson of Professor Max-Muller, who had married a Grenfell cousin. His first letter to Rivy is worthy of full quotation, for it shows the eagerness with which he plunged into a new life.

" I have fallen on my feet better than any cat, however low you dropped him. I went to stay with the Plesses, who are most kind. Princess Daisy has gone to London to Sunderland House, and you must go and see her. I said you would go and see her and help in anything she wanted. She is full of foreign politics, Anglo-German feeling, etc., and she is going to entertain and help Baron Marschall. She is a sort of Mrs. Astor over here, and makes me roar the way she gingers up the Deutschers. I stayed several days at Fürstenstein, a fine schloss with few valuable things in it,. but an enormous place with lovely scenery. They are very rich, and everything is done in great style—outriders, postillions, etc. They have fifty carriage horses, sixty riding horses, forty mares, three stallions, a lot of yearlings at Fürstenstein, and another stud at Pless.

" Unfortunately I did not see very much of Princess Daisy, as some Germans were there—the Governor of Silesia, a future Chancellor, they say. He talked French to me, and neither his French nor his looks impressed me very much. Then we all came back to Berlin to the Esplanade Hotel, where I have become a great swell through being of the Pless party. Here I have met two or three princes, the Foreign Minister under Bethmann-Hollweg, and many others.

" Pless, who ranks here as a sort of Duke of Devonshire, put me up at this Club [the Union], which is the best in Berlin. It is exactly like the Turf, except that every one talks to you, and at dinner every one dines at one table and there is a general conversation, all in German. To-night I sat next to Count von Bülow, the general in command of the Guard Cuirassiers. He asked me to go and see his cavalry brigade, and said he would show me everything. ' Such a pity I did not meet you yesterday, as my brigade was inspected, and you would have seen a good show.' The servants, food, and customs are the same as at the Turf, except that all the English papers are on the table, though I am the only Englishman here.

" From the above you will think I am living only in high life, but I am not. I found that the best university in Ger-

many is here, so, though it was not allowed, I plunged into
it. I do everything by myself, and have some amusing experiences through going to the wrong place at the wrong time.
I found there were lectures on every subject in the world,
and determined to attend. There are 5,000 undergraduates.
First I attended a lecture on the Saxon Invasion ot England.
I heard a lot of German, but did not understand anything.
I then thought to myself, ' Well, as I do not understand a
word, it doesn't much matter what the subject is; so, instead
of taking much trouble to find certain lecture rooms, I will go
into the first I come to.' 1 then followed about fifty students
into a room. The lecturer seemed to talk a bit different, and
on looking over the notes of the fellow next to me I found he
was talking Modern Greek ! To-day I went to a geography
lecture, arrived very late, plunged in and found a dead silence
and every one drawing. A professor came and spoke to me,
but neither could understand a word the other said. I went
to another lecture, but could not find out what it was about
from any source. In one hour I only caught the meaning of
one word, ' Pope Innocent.' Yesterday I stopped a student
in the passage and asked him to lunch with me, and begged
him to spout German, which he did. I said, ' I would like
to lunch where you usually go.' I found he was a vegetarian,
and we could only get carrots, etc. My bill, which I am going
to frame, was :—

Soup	1d.
Carrots and green peas	3d.
Sour Bulgarian milk .	2d.
Soda water . . .	½d.
	6½d.

I could not eat half the amount of carrots I was offered for 3d.
Students don't look half as smart as Porter [his servant], so I
now take him with me to the lectures. . . .

" Unfortunately I fall a little between two stools here, as
(1) if I am to learn the language, I must talk German ; if I talk

German, I can neither make myself understood nor understand anything the people say. (2) I can learn a good deal about Germany and go everywhere by talking English, as every one speaks English, and the few that don't, speak French. I cannot, therefore, learn the language and learn about Germany at the same time, so I am going to work hard at the language (I have every incentive to, as it is maddening not to understand a single word) and then go out again and mix in society, of which I am beginning to know the ropes. Every one has been extraordinarily kind and nice. The students, to whom I am an absolute stranger, go out of their way to show me what to do and where to go, and they do not even know my name."

From later letters I take some comments on German life and character.

" The opinion one gets of the Germans in England is a very wrong one. I expected to see a nation of magnificent physique, the Army superbly turned out, big soldiers and mighty clever men. The opposite is the case. These people are very ordinary, very much like us in character, with a great many good qualities and a large proportion of bad. The Guards I see are neither as smart nor as well turned out, nor to be compared physically with our Guards. Forty-five per cent. of the nation are rejected as soldiers through being too narrow or too blind. The shops give no credit to any one. They are unmethodically run, and are open for six and a half days without doing as much business as we do in five. The upper classes are narrow-minded and despotic ; the lower inclined to be boorish. They are by nature a rather suspicious people, but awful rot is talked about them in England. You travel just as easily as you do at home, and can see anything except inside a fort. They seem to be exactly opposed to the French, who appear excited but act coolly. These people appear very stolid, but get desperately excited the moment anything occurs. A row in the street and ten police

will yell without any leadership ; a row in a train and every
one starts screaming. . . .

"I am living fairly comfortably here, but getting rather
sick of cold pork and sausage. The table-cloth, too, is becoming a very intimate friend—it turns up so often. . . .

"I am not going to form any opinion until October, when
I will have had time for reflection. The Germans certainly
beat us, even our private soldiers, at drinking beer. I sat
next to a gentleman yesterday who drank five pints before I
drank one glass of water. He would have had a sixth, but
when the sixth was brought his wife took the glass and downed
it before him. The result is that a great many men and most
women are as fat as cattle. . . .

"I am enjoying every minute, as I rarely waste one. I
talk with tramcar drivers and conductors, taxi men, officers,
tennis pros, students, demi-mondaines, Berlitz teachers and
professors. Of course I lose a lot of what is said, but I have
picked up a good deal, and have as yet never received anything but the utmost courtesy and hospitality. I find I get
most out of taxi-drivers. They are either old soldiers, sailors,
invalids, or Socialists. I met one who had been in the German
South-West African war. He told me 400 men died in his
regiment, and the loss in the army was terrific through bad
water arrangements. Another was in the navy. He told me
many of the men are not half trained ; they bring men from
Würtemberg as conscripts who have never heard of or seen
the sea, and have in three years to be taught everything. I
personally cannot see how three years' service can make soldiers or sailors. . . .

"These people are very methodical but terribly slow.
They take ten hours to do what we do in six. I have not yet
seen much of the wonderful education of which we hear, and
have met a good many thick heads. Several officers have told
me they have not read a book for ten years. Germany, to
my mind, is not half what we think it is in England. Some
things are done very well, but I have seen a great many done
far better, and I am not half as impressed as I was with

America.   Nevertheless, I like these people.   The women—
Heaven save us from ever copying them! They are not
beautiful. . . .

" Berlin is one mass of demi-mondaines, cafés, restaurants—
one mass.   The great entertainment place is the Palais de
Dance.   It is most luxurious, and you might, if you did not
look at the women, think you were at a London ball.   The
women are most respectable-looking, but you can see that if
you want to dance you will get plenty of exercise, as once
round any of the dancers is equal to about twice round
Liverpool."

Germany revived Francis's interest in politics
and soldiering.   In July he wrote a long letter to
Mr. Churchill congratulating him on a speech
he had made.

" All the people I have seen appreciated very much its
straightforwardness.   The German character seems both to
understand and prefer plain speech to diplomacy.   They are
a very suspicious people.   They openly say that though they
understand that you spoke earnestly, they think you are un-
friendly.   They want to be very friendly, but on equal and
not on inferior terms as at present.   They openly talk of
going to war in the near future with France, partly from arro-
gance and partly from a craze so to weaken France that they
can diminish their military forces and increase their naval.
It does not look as if they would take on both France and
England together, and therein lies the hope of peace.   They
want to crush France on land and to be strong enough on the
sea to detain or delay a British army from landing on the Continent, so as to discourage British participation in a war between France and Germany.   My opinion of the Germans has
greatly declined since I came out here.   They are not as good
in quantity or quality as they represent themselves.   Their
character is to shake hands warmly and openly, but to keep

the other fist doubled in their pocket. . . . I am as certain that the Germans are riding for a fall as I am that you are riding to win."

In September came the Imperial manœuvres, that year held in Saxony, and Francis was determined to be present. The English representatives had already been appointed, so he was unable to go officially. Accordingly he hired a motor car and went as a spectator, giving a lift to a journalistic friend. When he arrived at the Bellevue Hotel in Dresden, he had a bad sick headache and went straight to bed ; so his friend filled up the police paper in which Francis's name was entered without his military rank. Unaware of this Francis sent a note to the cavalry barracks, saying he had a car and asking if any officer would like to go with him. This discovered to the police the fact that he was an English officer, and they promptly decided that he was a spy. The result was that a few days later, when he came back from watching the manœuvres, he found a police inspector in his room, who presented him with a letter saying that he must leave Dresden in twelve hours and Saxony in twenty-four. Francis was in a sad quandary, and, as was his practice on such occasions, he appealed straight to Cæsar. He remembered that he and Rivy the year before in London had shown some kindness to a son of the Saxon Chancellor, Baron Metzsch. Off went Francis to the Chancellor's house. The great man was not at home, but the Baroness received him warmly and asked him to breakfast the next morning. The matter was immediately straightened out. The police authorities laughed and shook hands, and Francis roamed throughout the rest of the manœuvres at his own sweet will.

In October he returned to England and put the result of his German experiences into a little pamphlet, which he printed privately and circulated to a number of friends. He returned to Germany for a short visit in December, and realized that his pamphlet, if it got about, might do him serious harm. On Mr. Churchill's advice he accordingly recalled all the copies. Its contents were simply an elaboration of what he had written in his letters. As it turned out, he had rightly diagnosed the trend of German feeling. " They are conscious of having attained such a position in the world that they resent being second to any, and they feel that the English block their way ; consequently they are not only jealous at heart, but can scarcely conceal their jealousy. No amount of pacific and philanthropic talk either in England or in Germany will prevent the latter from trying to get stronger and stronger, with a hope of some day being the foremost Power of the world. Even the Socialists would favour a war against France, because once France is crushed there is a chance of military service being less rigorous in Germany. . . . Careful observations convince me that if we wish to preserve peace it is necessary for us to be so strong that it will be impossible for the Germans to make war, as they would jump at any opportunity should they find us weak and isolated."

While Francis was in Berlin Rivy had been deep in polo, and had got badly bitten with ballooning. The year before he had made an airplane reconnaissance with Loraine during his yeomanry training, and in June Captain Maitland* took him up at Hurlingham in one of the new military balloons. They passed over Middlesex, Hertfordshire, Huntingdon, and Lincolnshire, and made an exciting landing six miles from Hull at 11.35 that night. A little later I find him writing to Francis suggesting that they should enter with Maitland for the long-distance ballooning record, at that moment held by the French. The year before Maitland had travelled 1,118 miles into the middle of Russia, and he now wanted to break the French record of 1,200 miles, starting in November when the westerly gales began. Nothing came of the scheme.

* Now Brig.-General Maitland, C.M.G., D.S.O.

Business took Rivy to Canada with his brother Arthur on 16th August. They travelled in a large party, and made a stately progress through the Dominion. I can only find one letter from Rivy during the tour, describing Sir Arthur Lawley's speech. " Joe Lawley made a speech on the responsibilities of Canada at Ottawa which brought tears to people's eyes, and made a very great impression. I will bring back a copy of it. It was by far the best speech that any of us had ever heard in our lives. I never realized he could do such a thing, and it made us very proud to think that we had an Englishman who could make such a speech, especially after Sir Wilfrid Laurier's very moderate effort."

In December of 1912 Arthur Grenfell had a bad horse accident, and Rivy found himself in consequence more closely tied to his office. In January 1913 the 9th Lancers went to Tidworth on Salisbury Plain, and in order that the brothers might spend their week-ends together, Rivy took the Red House in the neighbourhood, where he marked out a training ground for his polo ponies. In September 1912 Francis had been gazetted captain, and a little later was appointed adjutant. In the summer of 1913 he was working for the Staff College examination, and finally entered for it in great pain from a sprained ankle, which, taken in conjunction with the variety of his recent pursuits, made his success in qualifying the more remarkable. I find Francis writing to the King of Spain in January begging him to visit the 9th Lancers at Tidworth, and in any case to let his Military Attaché come and stay with them. " I can always give him horses or ponies to ride and introduce him to other officers of the garrison, including general officers, of which there are almost as many here as private soldiers. . . . Should you manage to come over to England for Cowes, my regiment is stationed only about forty miles from Southampton, and we could give you a good game of polo every day. You could motor over quietly and privately, and no one need know anything about it. Please keep this in mind, as a match between the 16th Lancers, with your Majesty playing, and the 9th Lancers, would make a fine combat. We have read with great interest about the reforms you have introduced in Spain, and the courage you have shown. It might well be said of Spain what Frederick the Great once said of England about Pitt, ' England, at any rate, has now a man at the head of affairs.' I am afraid it will not be possible for me to come over to Spain in the spring and enjoy the good sport we had two years ago. I am now adjutant, and find it hard to get away. We are very busy in case of a war, which we are quite ready for and looking forward to. If we go to war, as many Spanish officers as want to see it should join the 9th Lancers, for our one hope is to be in the advanced guard."

The year 1913 was passed pleasantly by both Twins in London and Tidworth, with such breaks as a trip to Paris with the Duke of Westminster at Christmas. Their real home was at Roehampton with their brother Arthur, for whom they had a deep affection. There among his children they seemed to be children themselves again. It was a period of that close companionship which for both was the main secret of happiness. I have never seen anything like their fidelity to each other. They had their own secret whistles and calls, and if either heard the other's summons it was his duty at once to leave whatever he was doing and obey it. In ordinary company they were just like two dogs. Francis would rise and leave the room, and Rivy would be apparently unconscious for some minutes of his departure. Then he would grow restless, and presently get up and saunter out to find his twin.

At this time they were most conspicuous figures in English society. They knew every one and went everywhere; and I fear that Rivy's devotion to letters must have declined, for with

his quicksilver brother at home he had small
opportunity for the studious life. But he did a
remarkable thing, which I think must be almost
unprecedented. To help Francis in his Staff
College work he took many of his classes with
him, read the same text-books, and went through
the same coaching. This must have been a real
effort, since at the time he was deeply engaged in
his brother Arthur's business and carrying many
new responsibilities. For the rest, both led the
varied and comfortable life which used to be the
perquisite of well-credentialled, reasonably rich,
and socially agreeable young men in England.
Each had the gift of oxygenating the atmosphere
in which he moved and waking a sense of life
in the flattest place. This was partly due, I
think, to the curious charm of their appearance :
they seemed always to be moving, or poised for
movement ; the ardour in their eyes was an anti-
dote for *ennui ;* they gave the impression of
never in their lives having been bored or idle.
Partly it sprang from their real ingenuousness.
They were acutely interested in everything in
the world, and refused to hide their interest after
the conventional English fashion. Often the
results were comic. They had vast stores of
ignorance, and would ask questions of an un-
believable *naïveté*. But comic or not it was a

most endearing trait, for it was perfectly natural, without pose or premeditation. It was this habit that especially attracted older men. Francis and Rivy were at their best with their seniors. Always respectful, they yet managed to treat an elder as if he were only a much wiser contemporary—one in whom the fires of youth were by no means dead. Their attitude was deferential in that it recognized superior wisdom, familiar since it assumed a comradeship in everything else. Also they revelled in " shop," and welcomed anybody who would tell them anything new. I have seen Rivy, with bright eyes, hanging on the words of an aged general, or banker, or professor, or quondam master of hounds, cross-examining him in an earnest quest for knowledge ; and the flattered face of the examinee showed how he relished the compliment.

To most of us the dividing line between the old and the new world was drawn in the first week of August 1914. But for the Twins it came earlier. Three months before the cataclysm of the nations they felt their own foundations crumbling. . . . Their brother Arthur's firm, in which Rivy was a partner, had had a career of meteoric brilliance, and had naturally aroused much jealousy among others who had entered for the same stakes. From 1912 onward it had been riding high speculative tides, where the hand of a skilled helmsman was badly needed. But Arthur's accident in the winter of that year kept him away from business for a considerable time, and when he returned it seemed to many of his friends that he was not the man he had been. Rivy had to deal on his own initiative with intricate matters which he probably never understood, for his business training had always been sketchy and inadequate. The affairs of the firm grew more and more involved, with the result that in the early months of 1914 a crash was imminent. In May the blow fell. The downfall of their brother's business involved every penny of the Twins' fortune.

This was the true tragedy of their lives, for the war brought no such bitterness. It meant that Rivy was a broken man in his profession, and that Francis must give up most of his ambitions. It made one's heart ache to see them, stunned, puzzled, yet struggling to keep a brave front, and clamouring to take other people's loads on their backs. Uncomplainingly they played what they decided was their last game of polo, and sold their ponies. Rivy was like one in a dream, trying to make out landmarks in an unfamiliar universe. Some terrible thing had happened, and by his fault—for his quixotic loyalty made him ready to shoulder all the blame —but he could not understand how or why. He was full of schemes to restore their fortunes, and I have rarely known anything so tragic as to listen to his schemes and endeavour to explain their bottomless futility. . . . It was a time when a man's friends are tested, and nobly most of their friends stood the trial. But there were others who, in the noonday of prosperity, had been ready to lick their boots, and who now invented slanders and gloated over the downfall. In my haste I considered that a public thrashing would have best met such cases ; but the brothers seemed to be incapable of anger. It was their gentleness that was so difficult to watch unmoved. They neither broke nor bent under calamity, but simply stood still and wondered. All that for fourteen years they had planned together had gone by the board, but they grieved about everybody's loss more than their own. It was the same with both : in that bad time they spoke and felt and thought with one spirit.

In the late summer of 1914 those of us who were trying against heavy odds to reach a settlement of the brothers' affairs were aware of a mysterious current moving throughout the world's finance, which thwarted all our efforts. Though we did not know it at the time, it was the first muttering of the great storm. By the middle of July it was clear that nothing could be done, and then suddenly that happened which submerged all personal disasters in a universal downfall. On Tuesday, 4th August, Britain sent an ultimatum to Germany, and at midnight entered upon war. What to most people was like the drawing in of a dark curtain was to the Twins an opening of barred doors into the daylight. For Francis the career which seemed at an end was to be resumed upon an august stage, and for Rivy the chance had come to redeem private failure in public service.

CHAPTER VII.

1914.

In 1909, when Francis went hunting north of the Zambezi, he travelled to the Victoria Falls with Colonel Marling, V.C., then Brigadier-General commanding the Potchefstroom district. He used to stare across the veld for hours at a time out of the window of the observation car, and once Colonel Marling asked what he was thinking about. " I was thinking how beautiful all this is," was the answer. " It makes me long to do something great." What makes the hero? Emerson asks, and replies,

> " He must be musical,
> Tremulous, impressional."

I never heard that Francis was musical, and he was about as tremulous as a brick wall. But he was always most sensitive to impressions, and in both the Twins a vein lay hidden of unspoken poetry. They now entered upon the struggle with a kind of awed and hushed expectation. It had long been at the back of their minds, and consciously and

unconsciously they had been preparing for it.
This little book is not a war memoir, for only a
fraction of the Twins' lives fell under the great
shadow—for Rivy about five weeks, and for
Francis less than ten months. But, looking back,
the war seems to have been always a part of their
outlook. Both had the standpoint of the regular
soldier ; neither suffered the hesitations and
divided impulses of the less fortunate civilian.
But their outlook in one sense was not the common
professional one—of the man who looks forward
to the practice of an art in which he has been
trained. Coming, as it did, to relieve them from
their perplexities, the crisis seemed to them to
carry with it a solemn trust, which they undertook
with willingness, indeed, but with something of
the gravity of those who feel themselves in the
hands of destiny.

The declaration of war found them together
at Tidworth. Rivy was determined to go out
with Francis, so he managed to get himself transferred from his proper unit, the Bucks Hussars,
as a reserve officer of the 9th Lancers. Every
moment of his time was devoted to sitting at
his brother's feet and learning what he could
teach him of the art of war, and to buying his
equipment with feverish haste. The Twins decided to take six horses between them, and they

borrowed an additional groom from the Duke of Westminster. " I am to take command of a squadron," wrote Francis in glee to Lord Grenfell. "My regiment was never better or more prepared in its history. . . . My dear old Uncle, you have been so kind to us that words to thank you fail me. If we survive you, we will look after your children and see that they get jolly well swished at Eton." On Thursday, 13th August, I find this note in his diary :—

" The Colonel [David Campbell] had dismounted parade at two o'clock. He made a splendid speech in which he recalled all the great deeds of the past which had been performed by the 9th : how in the Mutiny the regiment had carried out its duties and several officers obtained V.C.'s, with such distinction that when it left India the Viceroy gave orders that it should be saluted by forty-one guns. This had never been done before, and has never been done since. In Afghanistan it had been greatly praised by Lord Roberts ; in South Africa it fought for two years with the greatest distinction, and received the highest compliments from all its commanders. He also reminded us that Lieutenant Macdonald had on one occasion fought till every man and himself had been killed. He told us that we were going forth to the war with the greatest traditions to uphold. Nothing could be finer than his speech, or could possibly have appealed more to the officers and men."

The regiment embarked on the 15th. That morning Francis wrote to Lord Grenfell :—

" You will receive this when we have gone forth to war. We entrain to-day at 1 p.m., and hope to reach France to-night. We leave very quietly as if marching to manœuvres, but a more magnificent regiment never moved out of barracks for war. Every one is full of enthusiasm. Rivy goes with me, and it is a great thing having him. Good-bye, my dear Uncle. You have all my affection, and no one has ever been kinder than you have been to me during my lifetime. So far I have been the luckiest man alive. I have had the happiest possible life, and have always been working for war, and have now got into the biggest in the prime of life for a soldier. We will tell you some fine tales when we return with a bottle of the best from the Rhine."

That same day Rivy wrote to me—the last letter I had from him. " I cannot leave the country without writing to thank you, my dear John, for all you have done for me in our troubles. . . . Thank God, we are off in an hour. Such a magnificent regiment ! Such men, such horses ! Within ten days I hope Francis and I will be riding side by side straight at the Germans. We will think of you, old boy."

They got to Boulogne late on the evening of the 16th, and, passing through Amiens and Maubeuge, detrained at Jeunot in the afternoon of the 17th. The letters home from both during those days were very scrappy, consisting chiefly of references to the hard game of polo which they expected to play at any moment, and the close touch which they had established with the other players. Francis, however, kept a careful diary, and it is curious, considering what was to happen, that his main object seems to have been to record every moment which he spent with Rivy, and all that Rivy said or did. He was in command of "B" Squadron, and was determined to keep it up to the mark. Take, for example, this entry on 18th August: "I had reason to find fault with the turn-out of the men, boots and spurs having been allowed to get rusty; so I formed up the squadron and told them I insisted on the turn-out being good throughout the campaign, as it was proverbial that the best turned-out troop was nine times out of ten the best fighting one. I said that because the men were on active service there was no reason why they should imagine that they had ceased to be the Ninth and become colonials. I ordered the few men whose turn-out was very bad to march two miles on foot on the way home, and I told them in future that any man who was reported to me badly turned out would have his horse taken away from him and be made to tramp. I am certain that this had a great effect on the squadron."

From Jeunot the Ninth moved to Obrechies. "B" Squadron was the first cavalry unit to arrive, and naturally had a great reception from both French and Belgians. On the 19th and 20th it did a reconnaissance into Belgian territory,

and on Friday the 21st marched to Harmignies.
There Sir John French, it will be remembered,
was taking up position in advance of the left flank
of the French Fifth Army, preparatory to a move
against the German flank in Belgium. The presence of von Bülow's Second Army was fairly well
known, but there was more or less a mystery
about the whereabouts of von Kluck. He was
believed to be somewhere in the neighbourhood
of Waterloo, but neither the French nor the British
Staff had any guess at the strength of his forces,
or the great wheel which he was to undertake.
That Friday night the Twins were billeted in
Harmignies, and on Saturday the 22nd they
remained there till the evening, when the Ninth
were sent out to Thulin, where they arrived early
in the morning of the 23rd. They were now
behind the left flank of the British 3rd Division.

Francis and Rivy were much perplexed by
this strange kind of battlefield. As cavalrymen
they had hoped for the wide rolling downs which
had been predicted as the terrain of any con-
tinental war. Instead they found themselves in
a land full of little smoky villages, coal mines,
railway embankments, endless wire, and a popu-
lation that seemed as dense as that of a London
suburb. They were puzzled to know how cavalry
could operate, and they were still more puzzled

to understand what was the plan of campaign—
an uncertainty they shared with a million or so
other soldiers. On that hot Sunday morning
firing began early to the north-east and grew
heavier as the day advanced. In the afternoon
the Colonel sent for the squadron leaders and
told them that six German cavalry and three
infantry divisions were advancing, and that their
business was to retire slowly, fighting a rearguard
action. The rest of the day was spent in deep
mystification, with no knowledge of the fall of
Namur, or of Lanrezac's defeat at Charleroi, or
the other calamities which were to compel Sir
John French to retreat. But at 11.30 came definite
orders. They were instructed to entrench at the
railway station south of Thulin for an attack at
dawn. Spades were procured with difficulty, and
they were about to begin when another order
came not to entrench but to barricade, and to
hold Thulin station and the road to the south of
it. This was done, and the position was occupied
during the darkness, while the wretched inhabit-
ants straggled down the south road, and the guns
in the north grew steadily nearer.

Monday the 24th saw the beginning of the
retreat from Mons. This is not the place to
repeat an oft-told tale. Our concern is only with
one cavalry unit engaged in acting as a rear-

guard. At four o'clock that morning Francis, who had retired from Thulin at 10.30 the night before, was ordered to reconnoitre the town at dawn. He had gone only a little way through its streets when he came under heavy fire at short range, and in withdrawing had his horse " Ginger " shot down. Presently from his position at the railway station he saw a mass of German troops advancing. A sharp fight ensued of which he records, " Rivy and I found ourselves for the first time standing together under fire, and not much disconcerted." He had a bullet through his boot, and as the enemy was advancing in considerable numbers and outflanking the little post, " B " Squadron fell back upon the regiment, and was sent into reserve. The 9th Lancers then retired to a ridge more to the south, where they came under a heavy shell-fire.

It was now about midday. The 2nd Cavalry Brigade was south of Audregnies, with the exception of the 18th Hussars holding the high ground north of that village. The 5th Division was moving along the Eloges-Audregnies road. General De Lisle ordered the 9th Lancers to a position on the north-west of Audregnies, in order to support the 18th Hussars. There they assembled on a low hill where some shelter was obtained from buildings. The men were dismounted, and

(2,187)   13 firing at 1,200 yards against the German infantry, who were advancing deployed. Presently the retiring 5th Division, which had now been in action for some twenty-four hours, was threatened with an enemy envelopment, and Sir Charles Fergusson asked for protection from the cavalry for his western flank. De Lisle decided to charge the flank of the advancing masses, the 4th Dragoon Guards on the left and the 9th Lancers on the right.

That charge was as futile and as gallant as any other like attempt in history on unbroken infantry and guns in position. But it proved to the world that the spirit which inspired the Light Brigade at Balaclava and von Bredow's *Todtenritt* at Mars-la-Tour was still alive in the cavalry of to-day. . . . Francis formed his squadron in line of troops column, and they galloped into a tornado of rifle and machine-gun fire and the artillery fire of at least three batteries. No objective could be discerned, for the Germans at once took cover among the corn stooks. The ground had not been reconnoitred, and long before they came near the enemy the Lancers found themselves brought up by double lines of wire. In that nightmare place Francis's first job was to get his squadron in hand. He could not find his trumpeter, so he blew his whistle and cursed with vehemence anybody he found out of place. The charge had swung somewhat to the right. Captain Lucas-Tooth, commanding "A" Squadron, reached a high mound of cinders, and behind it and in a donga running eastward found shelter, and was presently joined by some of the 4th Dragoon Guards. Meantime Francis found a certain amount of cover behind a house. "We had simply galloped about like rabbits in front of a line of guns," he wrote, "men and horses falling in all directions. Most of one's time was spent in dodging the horses."

Very soon the house was blown to pieces, so the squadron moved off to the shelter of a railway embankment. Francis remembered that on one occasion the regiment had been ordered to trot in South Africa under a heavy fire, and he now adopted this method of keeping his men together. Under the embankment he collected the remnant. He found a number of odd 9th Lancers besides his own squadron, and as senior officer he took command and attempted to sort the troops out.

South of the embankment was the 119th Battery, R.F.A., under Major G. H. Alexander, who for this day's work was to receive the Victoria Cross. It was under a desperate fire from three of the enemy's batteries, one of which completely enfiladed it, and most of its gunners had been killed. Seeing the position, Francis offered his services. At that moment he was hit by shrapnel. " It felt as if a whip had hit me in the leg and hand. I think an artery was affected, as the blood spurted out, and my observer, Stead- man, and young Whitehead very kindly bound me up. We also had to put on a tourniquet, and referred to the Field Service Regulations to find out how it had to be put on. This would have amused you. Of course, we found out how to stop blood in every other part of one's body except one's hand, but eventually came upon this useful information. Things began to go round and round, and I luckily remembered that in the wallets of the horse I had borrowed I had noticed a flask. This proved to contain a bottle of the best old brandy, and my observer and I at once drank the lot. I now felt like Jack Johnson, instead of an old cripple."

Major Alexander asked Francis to find if there was an exit for his guns. The diary con- tinues the story.

" It was not a very nice job, I am bound to say, and I was relieved when it was finished. It meant leaving my regiment under the embankment and riding out alone through the guns, which were now out of action and being heavily shelled all the time, to some distance behind, where I found myself out of range of the shells. It was necessary to go back through the inferno as slowly as possible, so as to pretend to the men that there was no danger and that the shells were more noisy than effective. I reported to the Battery Commander that there was an exit ; he then told me that the only way to save his guns was to man-handle them out to some cover. My experience a few minutes before filled me with confidence, so I ordered the regiment to dismount in front of their horses, and then called for volunteers. I reminded them that the 9th Lancers had saved the guns at Maiwand, and had gained the eternal friendship of the gunners by always standing by the guns in South Africa; and that we had great traditions to live up to, as the Colonel had reminded us before we started. Every single man and officer declared they were ready to go to what looked like certain destruction. We ran forward and started pushing the guns out. Providence intervened, for although this was carried out under a very heavy fire and the guns had to be slowly turned round before we could guide them, we accomplished our task. We pushed out one over dead gunners. I do not think we lost more than three or four men, though it required more than one journey to get everything out. It is on occasions like this that good discipline tells. The men were so wonderful and so steady that words fail me to say what I think of them, and how much is due to my Colonel for the high standard to which he had raised this magnificent regiment."

According to Major Alexander, the enemy infantry were within 500 yards before the last gun was got out of shell range. Meantime Captain Lucas-Tooth had arrived, and being the senior officer took command of the regiment. " B " Squadron waited till all the battery had gone, and then, wrote Francis, " wandered about for some time looking for some one to give us orders." Eventually they halted by a main road along which an infantry column was marching. Here Francis was overcome by his wounds, and was forced to leave the squadron. It was now about seven o'clock. " The N.C.O.'s and the men came and shook me by the hand and gave me water from their water-bottles. I cannot tell you how much this day has increased the feeling of confidence and comradeship between me and my squadron. My fingers were nastily gashed, but the bone was not damaged ; a bit of shrapnel had taken a piece out of my thigh ; I had a bullet through my boot and another through my sleeve, and had been knocked down by a shell ; my horse had also been shot, so no one can say I had an idle day."

Room could not be found in any ambulance, so he was left by the roadside. Luckily a French Staff officer came by in a motor car and took him to Bavai. There he fell in with the Duke of Westminster, who took charge of him ; and he also found Rivy, who had been doing galloper to De Lisle. I quote again from the diary.

" They took me to a French convent, which was under the Red Cross and was full of wounded. A civilian doctor and six nurses attended me, each lady trying to outdo the others in kindness, which was rather alarming. There was a chorus of ' *Pauvre garçon ! Comme il est brave ! Comme il est beau !* ' The difficulty arose as to how my leg should be treated. I suggested my breeches should be taken off, but the senior

Red Cross lady said that that was impossible—' *Car il y a trop
de jeunes filles.*' So my breeches were cut down the leg. The
doctor took me to his house and put me to bed. I am bound
to say I felt rather done. I got into bed at ten o'clock. At
midnight Rivy told me to get up, as the town was to be evacu-
ated. The doctor gave me some raw eggs and coffee, and I
left Bavai at 1.15 a.m. in Bend Or's motor. I cannot say how
nice it was to find such a friend at such a time. It is wonderful
what Bend Or has done for Rivy and me. He took me to Le
Cateau, which we reached about four in the morning, where
I slept that day heavily in his bed. Next morning I heard of
the arrival of the 4th Division, and I also met Hugh Dawnay.
I left Le Cateau at 9 a.m. on the 26th in a cattle truck with
five other wounded. A very amusing thing happened in the
railway station. About 500 refugees were there, all in a great
state of distress and alarm, and a few gendarmes and soldiers.
Suddenly a German aeroplane came over. You would have
roared with laughter as all the refugees started yelling and
rushing about the station. Every gendarme or stray soldier
who possessed any sort of firearm loosed it off into the air,
which made the women yell all the more. A very fat officer
seized a rifle and rushed forward to shoot the aeroplane, which
was about five miles away. The bolt jammed, so he put it on
the ground, gave it a kick, and it went off through the roof.''

He reached Amiens safely that day, whence
he was transferred by way of Rouen to hospital
in England. He arrived very chastely dressed
in his regimental tunic and a pair of pyjamas,
his breeches having been sacrificed to the modesty
of the French nuns. I well remember how, out
of the confused gossip of those first weeks of war,
the exploit of the 9th Lancers emerged as a clear
achievement on which the mind of the nation

could seize and so comfort itself. For his work on that grim day Francis was recommended by Sir Charles Fergusson, the General commanding the 5th Division, for the Victoria Cross. The award was gazetted early in November, and so to Francis fell the distinction of being the first man in the campaign to win the highest honour which can fall to a subject of the King.

He was taken to Sister Agnes's hospital, and then to Mr. Pandeli Ralli's house in Belgrave Square. There he stayed a week, and afterwards went down to Lord Grenfell at Overstone. On 8th September he wrote to Rivy that he hoped to start back in a week for the front, though the doctors pretended that it might be a fortnight. He was desperately restless. " I am wondering what has happened to you in the meanwhile, and also to my squadron, as I am afraid you will have been having incessant fighting ever since I departed, and the strain must be very great. Even the little I went through practically knocked me up, and I have been in bed ever since." He was greatly embarrassed by his sudden fame, and he could not believe that he had done anything worth speaking about. " What a muddle it all was ! How I should have liked to see somebody who knew what was going on ! I have not yet discovered *what* we charged. All I saw was some infantry nearly a mile off." He had for the moment no pride in his exploit, only vexation at the fuss made about it. " Some infernal correspondents from France have written a lot of rot which makes me feel very uncomfortable. I have been bombarded with letters and telegrams from all over the place, and every sort of person has called to see me in hospital. I never felt such a fool in my life. After all, I only did what every other man and officer did who was with me. . . . The King came to see me in hospital, and was extraordinarily nice ; also Prince Arthur, who stayed an hour with me. Lord Roberts came and asked rather direct questions as to why we charged and whom we charged, and who gave the order to charge. . . . Mrs. Asquith came too, and asked after you. There is every sort of wild story about us, and a poem was even written in the *Times* on how we *captured the guns*. . . . Tell the officers to write on receipt of this, and I will bring out anything they want to them. Cable if you are all right."

That brief meeting in Bavai was the last time Francis saw his brother. During the afternoon of 24th August, when Francis and his squadron were charging the remote German infantry, Rivy had been acting as galloper for De Lisle. " A rather heavy job on a weary horse," he wrote. " He sent me to find General Gough, which I did; and the latter told me he had received no orders, and could not find Allenby, but since he had heard heavy guns in the direction of Eloges he intended to stay where he was. . . . We found Allenby about 11.30. He told De Lisle to go back and take the ridge from which we had been firing in the morning, but not to get too heavily engaged. De Lisle took his brigade back and sent the 18th Hussars about a mile north to a sugar factory, and followed himself, with me. Then I was sent to tell the 9th to wait north of Audregnies. As I gave the message an awful fire burst out from Quiveran. The Colonel told Abadie to hold the ridge. I had to gallop back across the line of fire to De Lisle, but when I had got there he had gone. The guns took up a hurried position behind the railway, but as they galloped to position a very heavy enemy fire was opened on them, the Germans soon finding the range. I went to the railway to look for De Lisle, and on approaching the ridge saw four artillerymen destroyed by shell. I then went round by the south bridge to find the 9th; but they, I was informed, had just charged. Meanwhile riderless and wounded horses were galloping everywhere, and bullets and shells were falling like hailstones.

. . . At last I found Colonel Campbell looking for the Brigadier to try and get some reinforcements. We found the Brigadier, but he had no troops with him. Colonel Campbell told me to stay with him. He had been ordered to charge towards Quiveran. Why, he did not know, as there was an open space for about a mile, and he had lost nearly all his regiment. . . . I was told to rally what force I could at Wiheries. I found some 4th Dragoon Guards, and then retired towards Athis with the Colonel. Afterwards we fell back, a very dejected force, to Bavai. I wondered how the devil I could get news of Francis."

Rivy's day's work, though he was the last man to admit it, was a very remarkable and courageous performance. Francis used to say that that solitary bit of reconnaissance, all alone, was braver than anything he ever did—a raw civilian riding for hours under heavy fire on a tired horse on missions of vital importance. That day established Rivy's reputation with the regiment. For the next ten days he was busy with the great retreat, and had very little time for letter-writing. On 29th August there was a short note to Francis telling him that both had lost all their belongings and begging him to bring out a new outfit. "An infernal trooper has bagged my horse with all my

kit on it, and has got lost himself." There was
a letter to one of his sisters, dated 2nd September,
and a postcard to Francis the next day, and after
that the next news was his death. In that feverish
fortnight David Campbell wrote : " Rivy was with
me as galloper and general utility officer up to the
time I left. He was of the very greatest help, and
carried out a very good reconnaissance with two
scouts the day before I was hit. He was always
splendid, and I shall miss him fearfully." On
5th September came the turn of the tide on the
Marne, and the Cavalry Corps moved northward
again. On the 7th the 2nd Brigade was acting
as flank guard to the division, with the 9th
Lancers as the advance guard ; and at Moncel
the Ninth, a troop and a half strong, led by David
Campbell himself, brilliantly charged with the
lance and dispersed a German squadron.

On 11th September the 2nd Brigade was on
the left bank of the Vesle river, and on the 13th
began the crossing of the Aisne by the British
infantry. The 9th Lancers, with the 4th Dragoon
Guards and the 18th Hussars, crossed the river
in advance near Bourg, and pushed up the heights
towards Vendresse. There they were relieved by
a battalion of the infantry advance guard, the
60th Rifles, and retired for the night to Pargnan.
On the morning of the 14th the Ninth again

formed the advance guard, and leaving at 3 a.m. marched north by Vendresse and Troyon. They had been given an objective which turned out to be about a mile behind the German trenches. Pushing fast through the dark up a winding road towards the Chemin des Dames, they passed the pickets of the 60th, and presently ran into a German picket. The regiment dismounted, while Rivy, with a section, dashed forward to a position near a haystack. He engaged the enemy picket, and enabled the regiment to regain its direction.

He seems to have been in wild spirits, and to have encouraged his little band with jokes, and with that peculiarly cheery hallo of which he had the secret. But, in his anxiety to see the effects of the shots, he exposed himself, and a German bullet cut his revolver in two and passed through the roof of his mouth. He died instantaneously. The last words which his men remember were his shout, " Steady your firing, boys. We have got them beaten."

The Ninth fell back, leaving his body in the enemy hands, but that afternoon the 60th advanced and recovered it. Rivy had been in the field twenty-five days—days of such crowded endeavour and endurance as few campaigns in history can show. From the first hour he had been supremely happy, for he had found his true calling. He had seen his brother safe out of danger and covered with glory, and with the removal of any anxiety about Francis had gone the one thing which could dim his cheerfulness. From what I have been told by his men and his brother officers, I am certain that that last fortnight of his life had washed clean from his mind all the weary sense of reproach and futility which had been clouding it, and that he went to death as one who " finds again his twentieth year."

CHAPTER VIII.

1914–1915.

"Tarry, dear cousin Suffolk!
My soul shall thine keep company to heaven;
Tarry, sweet soul, for mine, then fly abreast,
As in this glorious and well-foughten field
We kept together in our chivalry!"

IT took Francis a long time to realize that Rivy was dead. He was about to return to the battle line; death was everywhere; already many of his friends had fallen; he himself might follow at any moment; his mind was a little dulled to the meaning of mortality. He did not think of the blankness of his future without Rivy, for there was no reason to expect that it would be long. His predominant thought was how splendid his brother had been in life and how glorious in death, and he wanted every one to realize this. But the acute personal loss had not yet come home to him. Of the many letters which he received, I think he was most touched by that of the King of Spain :—

"DEAR FRANCIS,—I never knew that Rivy had joined the Ninth. I thought he belonged to the Yeomanry. You cannot imagine what a blow it has been to me, and I can guess what you must feel. We followed all the fine work you did, and Bend Or's coming to your rescue, and I was sure that I would be able to drink with you both on your V.C. I never would have believed that Rivy would have died before me, and he a civilian. Do write when you can, old man, and tell me everything. Please give your brothers and sisters all my sympathies. I have lost a friend, and I can only tell you that he has found the finest of deaths: he died for his country on the battlefield. You are a soldier, and know what I mean. You know that I am no good at making phrases, so good-bye, old man. I hope you will recover soon. Believe me always your devoted friend,   ALFONSO."

To Lord Grey Francis wrote :—

" I wired to you on Saturday when I heard the news, for you were one of his best friends. Rivy died for old England, and no Englishman could do more. We won the Champion Cup together, and I bought him the horse on which he won the Kadir, and we have been through good times and bad, and on the 24th of August we went into action together and faced the bullets side by side. We have worked, played, and fought together, and always shared everything. After thirty-four years of inseparableness it was on the battlefield that we parted, and only death—the most glorious death of all—has now compelled us to separate for ever, at any rate in this world.

" My dear Lord Grey, you were a very, very good friend to Rivy, and you and your family have done all you could to enrich and ennoble his life. He dearly loved you all, and valued nothing more in the world than your friendship, and admired nothing more than your character. I hope that since we can no more talk of the ' Twins ' you will always remember Rivy and accept the gratitude of your broken-hearted friend."

And to me :—

> " Rivy's death will hit you as hard as it has hit me. He
> was so very fond of you. You were his most loyal friend, my
> dear John, and I hope you will accept the great gratitude of
> his twin, and whenever you think of Rivy I hope you will say
> to yourself, ' He knew I always stood by him through thick
> and thin.' "

Rivy for him was still a living personality, separated only by the exigencies of warfare ; and he
wanted all their friends to think of him and talk
about him, and not merely hold him in pious
memory, as if by some such affectionate concentration of thought he could be recaptured from
the pale shades.

Meantime he was on tenterhooks to be back
at the front, and on the evening of 8th October
he left England to rejoin his regiment. At the
moment the British army was moving to the
extreme left of the Allied line, in the hope of
turning the German northern flank. He travelled
with his Colonel, David Campbell, who had now
recovered from his wound got on the Marne.
On the 12th he found the regiment at Strazeele,
and to his delight discovered that it was on the
verge of going into action. To be among his old
friends again both soothed and cheered him.
" Several still call me Rivy," he wrote to his
uncle. " I am so glad it goes on."

The 1st Cavalry Division, now under De
Lisle, to which the 2nd Brigade belonged, was
engaged in reconnoitring the ground in front of
General Pulteney's 3rd Corps. Pulteney's business was to get east of Armentières, astride the
Lys, and to link up Smith-Dorrien at La Bassée
and Haig at Ypres. The enemy was in Merris
and Meteren, and the 9th Lancers were drawn
up at Strazeele, while the 4th and 6th Infantry
Divisions attacked. It was a day of heavy rain
and thick steamy fog, the fields were water-
logged, aircraft were useless, and the countryside
was too much enclosed for cavalry. The infantry
succeeded in their task, and by the morning of
the 14th Pulteney held the line Bailleul-St. Jans
Cappelle. Francis notes in his diary : " I could
not help observing on my return that the war was
affecting the spirits of all a little : there was much
more seriousness than when I left."

The stage was now set for that First Battle of
Ypres which was to last for three weeks between
Dixmude and La Bassée,—which will live in history as one of the greatest military achievements
of Britain, and which was at once the end and
the apotheosis of the old British regular army.
On the 15th Francis took over " B " Squadron
again, and told the men how glad he was to get
back to them, and how proud he was to hear of

the way in which they had behaved since he last
saw them. He told them that the war would be
long, and that this was not the time for any man
to count his losses. That day he marched through
a steady rain to Locre. The next day, starting
very early, he marched through Ploegsteert village
and Ploegsteert Wood ; and at Le Gheir was instructed to attack and carry the Lys crossing at the
bend of Pont Rouge. The squadron took the village, but found the bridge strongly barricaded, and
the enemy entrenched on the far side of the stream.
Francis asked permission to swim the river, and
when this was refused he begged for reinforcements so as to carry the barricade. To his disgust, however, he received orders to retire. " Before leaving we buried Private Lake at a farm 800
yards south of the Pont Rouge. Owing to our
nearness to the enemy we had to carry on the
burial service in the dark, which was not nice.
At the service I said, ' Here lies a brave British
soldier who has died for England and the 9th
Lancers, and no man could do more.' Then I
said the Lord's Prayer, and afterwards thought
of the poem to Sir John Moore."

Next day " B " Squadron was in reserve, and
was consistently shelled all day ; very disquieting
for cavalry, who had to think of their horses.
On the 18th Francis was at Le Gheir again,

and " B " Squadron was once more instructed
to attack Pont Rouge with infantry support.
The aim was to clear the right bank of the Lys,
for Pulteney was still doubtful about the strength
of the enemy, and had some ground for assum-
ing that the only Germans there were the mixed
cavalry and infantry he had been pressing back
for a week. As a matter of fact the 3rd Corps
was now approaching the main German position,
and in spite of the brilliant work of the cavalry
could not win the right bank of the river. Pulteney was firmly held at all points from Le Gheir
to Radinghem, and his position on the night of the
18th represented the furthest line held during the
battle by this section of our front. Francis's fight
on the 18th was much the same as that on the
16th. " B " Squadron could not get near its
objective because of the machine-gun fire, and
was only extricated by the aid of two companies
of Inniskilling Fusiliers.

It was now necessary to connect Pulteney with
the infantry further north, and a link was provided
by the whole Cavalry Corps under Allenby. On
the night of the 19th Allenby was generally east
of Messines on a line drawn from Le Gheir to
Hollebeke. On the 20th Francis found himself
on the Messines Ridge supporting the 4th
Dragoon Guards, who were holding St. Ives.

Here they had another ugly scrap, and late in the evening had to support the Household Cavalry at Warneton. The day before he had written to his uncle : " This war is damnable. We have such nasty jobs to do, and are always under fire ; but the spirit of the men is splendid. Our infantry and cavalry outclass the German, but their artillery is excellent. Our present job is pretty disheartening. We go forward and capture positions for the infantry, who are entrenched four miles behind and move terribly slow. We are then withdrawn, and have again to recapture the same position next day. Eventually the infantry come up and take the place, assisted by divisional artillery—the same place we took three days before with a squadron."

The 9th Lancers were gradually being transformed from cavalry to infantry, and a passage in Francis's diary shows how severe were the duties. " We have started the same old game as at the Aisne, and we have had five of the hardest days of the war in trenches repelling German attacks. It has become such a recognized idea to use us for this work as soon as we get in touch with the enemy that I am afraid all the cavalry traditions are for ever ended, and we have become mounted infantry pure and simple, with very little of the mounted about it. Our men look funny sights trudging along with spades and things on their backs, and when they are mounted they look funnier still : if you see a man carrying lance, sword, rifle, spade and pick, he looks just like a hedgehog. But it is a jolly hard life for them to have to fight their way up to the line, then make the line, then hold it, and all the time cleaning and trying to look after their horses." " Do you know any one who would send me an armoured motor car with a Maxim ? " he wrote to his uncle. " I have written to Winston that the thing would be invaluable now."

On the 21st and 22nd the regiment was engaged on the Messines Ridge in support of the 5th Cavalry Brigade. On the 23rd they were actually at Messines, then still the semblance of a village, with its church still a church and not yet a ragged tooth of masonry. The cavalry were holding a trench line to the east of the place, where they were most completely and continuously shelled. On the 26th they were sent south to support Smith-Dorrien's 2nd Corps in the fighting around Neuve Chapelle. It was a critical moment, for the 7th Infantry Brigade, which had been in action for eighteen days, had been forced back west of Neuve Chapelle and had almost ceased to exist as a fighting force. That day an attempt was made to recapture the village. The

attack was too weak to succeed, and the most that
could be done with the assistance of the cavalry
was to take up a good defensive position on the
west. On the 29th the 9th Lancers were back
at Neuve Eglise, behind the Messines position.
That experience gave Francis his first notion of
the real seriousness of the German attack. Before,
he had been confident, and had credited every
optimistic rumour ; now he saw that the enemy
was indeed flinging the dice for victory, and that
the scanty British forces were faced with pre-
posterous odds.

On 29th October, as we know, began the critical stage of the First Battle of Ypres. The chief
danger points were at the apex of the salient
around Gheluvelt and on its southern flank about
Zillebeke. But there was also an attack at the
southern re-entrant, and heavy fighting along the
whole Messines Ridge. On the 30th the 1st
Cavalry Brigade was holding the line before
Messines, and the 9th Lancers were sent up in
support. Francis's squadron, however, was de-
tached to assist the 4th Cavalry Brigade at Wytschaete. Allenby, it must be remembered, at the
time was holding the whole line from Klein Zillebeke to the south of Messines, and he had no reinforcements except two much-exhausted battalions
of an Indian brigade from the 2nd Corps. The

British public, who compared a cavalry regiment to an infantry battalion and a cavalry squadron to an infantry company, forgot the disparity in numbers. A cavalry regiment was only 300 strong as against 1,000 men of an infantry battalion, and a squadron only 46 as against 200 of an infantry company.

That day Francis's work lay in entrenching a position in the Wytschaete neighbourhood. In the evening he was sent for to report to his Colonel at Messines. He arrived there to find the situation growing desperate. The front north of the village was becoming untenable. He took his squadron to the old trenches east of Messines which it had occupied two days before. It was now only 40 men strong—far too few to hold the ground. All the night of the 30th he was heavily fired on, and the enemy could be seen moving about on his left flank. He found his Colonel, and showed him the danger of the position. The most that could be done, however, was to throw back a trench on the left at a sharp angle to prevent outflanking.

Saturday, 31st October, was the crisis of the battle. It saw the menace to the Salient itself repelled by one of the most heroic exploits in our record, but it also saw the end of Messines. The events of that day are best told in an extract from Francis's diary.

" After an anxious night, in which I did not sleep at all, we stood to arms, and were ready for the attack which came in due course at daybreak. At about five a.m., quite close to us, I heard horns blowing and German words of command and cheering, and I knew that the Germans had attacked the Indians on our right. Basil Blackwood came and told me the Colonel wished me to send two troops to support the right at once, and I sent Mather Jackson and Sergeant Davids. The latter I consider to be one of the bravest men in the British army, and regarded him as the backbone of my squadron. I regret to say that was the last time I saw him, as during the attack he was badly wounded and captured by the Germans. During the night, when I felt anxious, he was so calm that I went and consoled myself by a talk with him. We discussed the principles of fighting, and he said that the principles on which he acted were that if you were killed by a shell it was just bad luck, but that in an attack he considered himself as good as any German, and it was only a question who got the first shot in. He was very quiet throughout the night— in fact at one moment I had to do a lot of kicking at him to wake him when I thought the position serious.

" I was now left with two very weak troops—that is, from 15 to 20 men and a machine gun. Suddenly, about twenty yards to our rear at daybreak there was a rush of men from some houses. To my utter astonishment they appeared to be Germans. Apparently the enemy had done what we thought he would do during the night : he had got round my extreme left, and unfortunately, instead of attacking me he had attacked the troops on my left, who had given way. The Germans were therefore round us at a distance of 100 yards. They took a house, ran up to the top storeys and fired straight into my trench. Poor Payne-Gallwey, who had only joined two nights before and was in action for the first time, was shot in the head from behind and killed. Reynolds was shot through the head, and several more were wounded. I was on the extreme right of the trench when this was reported to me. I had decided to hang on when I became aware that ' C ' Squadron, who were in front and could protect my front, had received orders to withdraw. At this moment heavy fire was directed on our trench, not only from the rear but also from the left flank, where the Germans had brought up a machine gun. Luckily the bullets went a bit high. I ordered the men to retire from the right and crawl out of the trench to the houses that were on their right in the brickfield. When I got there I met Major Abadie, who said to me, 'Well, Francis, what do you think of the situation?' I cannot remember exactly what I said, but I think I told him that I thought the Germans were attacking from front and left, and that I had no trench facing that way to meet the attack, the troops on my left having gone away. This was the last I saw of him. He looked exactly the same as usual and was in the same cheery mood, taking everything light-heartedly, as was his custom.

" I now waited in a ruined house in the rear of the first barricade, and am bound to say I felt in a quandary as to what to do. I felt very guilty at leaving my trench, but at the same time I felt it was useless to hold it. . . . Suddenly I heard a machine gun still firing at the extreme end of our old trench. It had been left behind, so I left the squadron at the house and went back along the trench until I reached the gun, where I found Corporal Seaton with another man in action, the Germans being from 20 to 40 yards off. I told him I thought he had better retire, and that I would help him out with his gun ; but he said that as the man with him was wounded, and something had gone wrong with the gun, he thought it best to leave it behind and completely disable it. He retired along the trench. I remained there awhile, firing at Germans with my revolver. My firing was not very steady, and although I could see Germans lying down quite close I could not take careful aim, as I was being shot at from front, flank, and rear. I picked up one or two rifles to fire with, but they jammed. I then realized that this was no place for the squadron leader, so crawled along the trench and rejoined my squadron near the ruined house.

" Here I received orders to hang on, and was told that

'C' Squadron, under Major Abadie, had been ordered to attack the house in our rear with the bayonet. I was again in a dilemma what to do, but pulled myself together, hoping I should be inspired to do the right thing. The only inspiration I got was a sort of feeling within me to go back and hold my trench, so I assembled the squadron and told Mather Jackson and Frank Crossley that I proposed to reoccupy the trench. They thought this might be difficult, as the Germans seemed to have got into the end of it. However, feeling that it was the right thing to do, and confident that we should get from traverse to traverse as quickly as the Germans, and that I could fire in front quicker with my revolver than they could with their rifles, we went back to the trench and reached the extreme end of it. After being there a few moments the officers reported that we were being shot at from front and rear. I ordered them to tell the odd numbers to fire to the front and the even numbers to fire to the rear and to hang on. I went to the extreme left of the trench, where I could see the left flank. There I could see some Germans running back, but about a thousand yards off one or two German companies advancing, covered by skirmishers in excellent order. We picked up at least six rifles to fire at them, but they all jammed.

"I again felt uncertain what to do. Our position seemed really ridiculous—most of our rifles having jammed, and the Germans all round. I sent word back to 'C' Squadron to advance as quickly as they could against the house, saying we should cover their advance from where I was; but they replied that it was impossible for them to move. As the only use I could be at this time in my trench was to cover the advance of 'C' Squadron, I decided to leave it again, and assembled the squadron under heavy artillery and machine-gun fire near the ruined house. I found the Colonel, and told him the situation. He told me we were to hold on at all costs. He said that infantry were advancing to support us, but could not be up for some time—I think he said two o'clock. He told me to hold the small ridge facing north, and reinforced me with two troops of the 5th Dragoon Guards. I went back, and on the way spoke to Lennie Harvey, who was standing with his troop in the road. I also passed Raymond Greene. I told Lennie Harvey I had had orders to hold the ridge, which I pointed out to him, and told him to hold the ridge on my left. This, I believe, is the last that was seen of that officer. . . . We were now being very heavily shelled by coal-boxes, and it really seemed as hot as any one could wish for. There seemed to be nothing in the air but shells, and the bursting of the coal-boxes made a most terrific noise. Personally, I had the feeling which I have had before, the same as one gets at the start of a steeplechase, when the starter says ' Off.'

" At this moment a shell pitched right into the middle of my squadron and blew it to the winds. Several of the men were very badly wounded—especially Corporal Newman, to whom I gave some morphia. I myself was hit through the leg, and felt I could not move. Luckily for me Mather Jackson and another man took hold of me and carried me back. On the way we passed Beale Brown and told him what had happened—that the front of the town was untenable owing to the shells, and that all that could be done was to attack the Germans on our left. I was then carried back to the second barricade, where I met Charles Mulholland and also General Briggs, to whom I explained the situation. Mulholland took me to a house where the 11th Hussars' doctor was, and I was taken down to the cellar, where there were a lot of wounded. After I had had some rum and my wound dressed I was sent through the town to an ambulance, which took me to Bailleul.

" On arrival at Bailleul a terrible fire suddenly opened in the streets, which was very alarming to us caged in the ambulance. Luckily it proved only to be firing at an aeroplane. We were taken to a convent, and my stretcher was put down, curiously enough, alongside Basil Blackwood and Jack Wodehouse. Basil Blackwood and I, I have since heard, were the only two to escape that day from Messines."

Francis's second wound was a serious one in the thigh. He was sent to Dublin, and complained that after a journey of two nights he was farther from England than when he started. " I am in a home," he told his uncle ; " very comfortable, indeed, in a room with two others. The nurses are quite splendid. The surgeon has done our dressings much better than anything before and made us all comfortable. In addition to this every one in Ireland has been to see us. Our room is so thick with flowers it is hard to breathe. Ivor Wimborne has fitted us all out with glorious pillows, razors, brushes, etc. I could not possibly be more comfortable or in better hands."

On the 17th he read in the *Gazette* the news of his Victoria Cross. " I have been through so much since June," he wrote to his uncle, " that what would and should have made me yell with joy nearly causes tears. It gave me no great feeling of having achieved anything. I feel that I know so many who have done and are doing so much more than I have been able to do for England. I also feel very strongly that any honour belongs to my regiment and not to me. They have paid the toll, and will go on paying until the road is clear. . . . My dear uncle, without the help of Providence how futile our efforts are ; but with it even humbugs like myself can masquerade as brave. It will be a lifelong pleasure and honour to your nephew to know that you, one of the greatest soldiers of our time, who have done so much for our name and have been so kind to Rivy and me, should have lived to see this day. Indeed, the greatest joy of all is that it will please you."

For five months he remained in England, and the first three were, I think, the hardest trial of his life. He was slow to get well, and limped about London with a thin face and haggard eyes, looking like a man searching for something which he could not find. Now he realized what his brother's death meant to him. The alliance of thirty years was broken for ever, and he had lost half of himself. His looks at that time used to frighten me : he had the air which in Scotland we call "fey," as if the "waft of death " had gone out against him. He forced himself to be cheerful, but his gaiety was feverish and his old alacrity had died. I remember that he tried to interest himself in the general conduct of the war and would argue eagerly for a little—and then suddenly fall silent. For things more poignant than tactics and strategy crowded his mind. He never doubted our ultimate victory, but meantime Rivy was dead and every day his friends were dying, and it seemed as if the price of victory would be the loss of all that he had loved.

He was miserable, too, at being away from his regiment and his squadron. No man who has not served in a unit in the field can understand the intimate ties which bind together its members. It is so small and so forlorn—a little clan islanded amid great seas of pain and death. The regimental tradition becomes a living thing like a personal memory. Old comradeships in sport and play and the easy friendliness of peace-time are transformed into something closer even than friendship. Every communal success becomes an individual triumph, every loss an individual sorrow. More than most regular officers Francis had this aching affection for his regiment—the devotion of " a lover or a child." At Christmas he sent this message to his squadron :—

" I wish you all the very best of luck and good wishes for Christmas and the New Year. I am always thinking of you, and hope very soon to return. Sir John French said the regiment had exceeded the greatest traditions of the army, and in this ' B ' Squadron has played the leading part. You were the first squadron of the regiment in action at the beginning on 24th August, and have since always given the lead. Remember the brave that have fallen, and be determined to serve England as faithfully as they.

" You have all my very, very best wishes and thoughts. God bless you and keep you, and help you to remain the finest squadron in the world—the only squadron that has got for itself already a D.C.M., a Legion d'Honneur, a commission, and a V.C., for what is won by the leaders belongs to the men. God bless you all."

Slowly, very slowly, his wound mended, and he began to look more steadily upon the world. Old friends, such as Mrs. Asquith and Lord Hugh Cecil, did much to restore his balance; and when he went to spend Christmas with his brother Arthur, who was training with the Bucks Yeomanry in Norfolk, he was beginning to be himself again. In January 1915 he took up shooting, for which he had never greatly cared, and discovered that on occasion he could be a brilliant shot. Then he advanced to hunting at Oakham on Harry Whitney's horses, and in March he reported to his uncle that he was " a fighting man once more." " It is glorious to feel strong and well, but I am bound to say the stronger and better I get the more I seem to realize what it means to have lost Rivy." And he adds a characteristic note : " I am glad to say my nerve has gone—in the right direction. Fences are not as frightening as bullets. It is a joke to be afraid of things that are there to shelter cattle and not to kill you." He had been suffering from too clear a perspective, seeing human effort too constantly against the cold background of eternity. Now he could look upon life in partitions, and accept the kindly conventions which humanity has devised to shelter it from the outer winds. Therefore, as he put it, he became "keen" again; for keenness means that the mind is fixed on the various *stadia* of the game of life, and not on the horizon.

When he was passed fit for foreign service he made a new will, appointing the late Lord Grey and myself his executors and trustees. His affairs were very complicated, and it was by no means certain that he had much or anything to leave; but with characteristic optimism he made elaborate dispositions among various members of his family. He left his medals to his regiment, "to whom the honour of my gaining the Victoria Cross was entirely due, thanks to its splendid discipline and traditions." I quote the last two clauses.

"I wish to express my regret that my financial position does not permit me to leave anything to the children of my uncle, Francis, Lord Grenfell, as I had hoped to do, but I should like to express to him my deep gratitude for his kindness to me during my lifetime. Ever since the day when he decided that I should go into the army at his expense I have endeavoured to base my career on his example. He has, since the death of my father, done everything that a father could do for me. I should also like to thank all my brothers and sisters for their kindness, generosity, and hospitality to me. No junior member of a family could have been blessed with more happy relations.

"I should like everything possible done at all times for mine and Rivy's friends, notably the Hon. Mrs. Arthur Crichton,

Mrs. Duggan, the Countess of Erne, the Countess of Dudley, Lord Francis Scott, Lord Grey, the Hon. Angus McDonnell, Mr. and Mrs. Waldorf Astor, Mrs. Brooks, the officers of my regiment, including Brig.-General Campbell (who has stood by me in peace and war on every single occasion), Mr. and Mrs. Strawbridge, Captain Clowes, the Earl of Rocksavage, and the many others who have on all occasions stood by me and to whom I am deeply grateful. My special thanks are due to the Duke of Westminster for his great generosity and kindness to me on many occasions. No man ever had a better friend. I owe a great deal of gratitude to my servants, who have served both my brother and myself most loyally for a long time. Without making any legal obligations, I would like my family to do what they can to assist the Invalid Children's Aid Association, as my brother Rivy asked me."

On 7th April he gave a farewell dinner at Claridge's. It is an occasion I can never forget, for it was the last time I saw him, and it seemed to me that he had recovered and more than recovered all his old ardour and youthfulness. The party were his brother Arthur, Lord Grenfell, Reggie Barnes, Mr. Arthur Balfour, Mr. Winston Churchill, Mr. Andrew Weir (now Lord Inverforth), and myself. It was on that occasion, I remember, that Mr. Churchill first expounded his views about those instruments of war which were to develop into the Tanks. The discussion roamed over the whole field of military and naval policy, and I have rarely heard better talk. Some of the best of it came from Francis, and I realized how immensely his mind had ripened and broadened in the past months. I began to think that if he were spared he would be not merely a gallant leader of troops but a great soldier.

Francis rejoined his regiment on Wednesday, 21st April. He found the 9th Lancers in billets at Meteren, where they had been training on and off for several months. " I must say," he wrote, " I am mighty glad to get back here, for this life is made for me. . . . I find pals everywhere. I somehow never seem to go anywhere out here without finding friends." Next evening orders suddenly came to saddle up and support the French north-east of Ypres. In the April twilight a strange green vapour had appeared, moving over the French trenches. It was the first German gas attack, and with it the Second Battle of Ypres began.

The 1st Cavalry Division marched through Poperinghe to the canal, and for two days supported the French on the extreme left of the battlefield. The Ninth were lucky enough to have no casualties, and on the Sunday they returned to their quarters at Meteren. A week later, on 2nd May, when the second great German attack was delivered, they were moved into reserve behind the Salient. On the 6th they were in Ypres itself, and on the 7th they were back in

Meteren, under the impression that their share in the fight was over.

Those who remember the Salient only in the last years of the campaign, when it had become a sodden and corrugated brickyard, can scarcely conceive what the place was like during the throes of the Second Battle. The city of Ypres was dying, but not yet dead, and its solemn towers still stood, mute protestants against the outrage of war. To the east of it the meadows were still lush and green, and every hedgerow and garden bright with lilac, laburnum, and guelder-rose. It was a place of terror, but also a place of blossom. The sickly smell of gas struggled with the scent of hawthorn; great riven limbs of flowering chestnuts lay athwart the roads; the cuckoo called continually from the thickets. The horror of war seemed increased a thousandfold when shells burst among flowers, and men died in torture amid the sounds and odours of spring.

On 3rd May the British line had been shortened, and on the 12th it was possible to relieve the 28th Division, which had been fighting continuously for twenty days. Its place was taken by a cavalry detachment—the 1st and 3rd Cavalry Divisions under De Lisle. Their front ran from the Frezenberg ridge southward across the Roulers railway to the Bellewaarde Lake north of Hooge.

Francis, who had been uneasy waiting behind the line, welcomed the change. " Here we are," he had written, " sitting peacefully behind like the next man to go in to a fast bowler. You don't want to go in, and yet you would like to be knocking about the bowling." His brigade took up position in the front line late on the evening of the 12th. The trenches had been much damaged, and it was necessary to reconstruct the parapets and traverses.

Thursday, 13th May, a day of biting north winds and drenching rains, saw one of the severest actions of the battle. The German bombardment began at three a.m., and in half an hour parapets were blown to pieces, and the whole front was a morass of blood and mire. The heaviest blow fell on the 3rd Cavalry Division south of the Roulers railway, but the 1st Division did not escape. Its two brigades in line, the 1st and 2nd, were able to maintain their ground, but it was by the skin of their teeth. The 9th Lancers' front was held by " C " Squadron, under Captain Graham, on the left, and " B " Squadron, under Francis, on the right. On the left were the 18th Hussars, whose trenches were utterly blown to pieces. A gap presently appeared there, but the advancing enemy was stopped by machine-gun fire from a fortified post which Captain Graham

managed to create in the nick of time. All day
the battle lasted, and by the evening the right
of the cavalry front towards the Bellewaarde
Lake sagged backward. During the early night
the bombardment revived, and it was the turn
of " B " squadron to have their right flank exposed.
The situation, however, was saved by the oppor-
tune arrival of the 11th Hussars. At one a.m.
on the morning of the 14th the Ninth were relieved,
and went back to water-logged trenches in front
of Ypres, whence late that evening they were
withdrawn to Vlamertinghe. They had lost 17
killed and 65 wounded, and " B " Squadron 16
killed and 30 wounded, including all troop leaders
and sergeants.

Francis's part in the great fight is only hinted
at in his diary. " The most fearful bombardment
lasted for fifteen hours. It is wonderful how one
escapes. These cursed coal-boxes burst all down
the trench, but often missed us, often only by two
or three yards, but that makes all the difference.
Whatever is in store for the future, I shall never
be nearer death than I was on the 13th. The
spirit of the men was simply splendid. No one
dreamed of retiring, and when some Huns began
advancing there was a cheer of ' Hurrah! at last we
shall get our own back ! ' Unfortunately one of
our own shells pitched near them, and they ran like

hares. Oh, dear! What a lot of friends I have
lost." He mentions casually that during the whole
battle he "felt keen and never lost confidence."
Indeed he seems to have behaved throughout as
if he were having a good day in the Shires. Francis
in war had much of Lord Falkland's quality, as
recorded by Clarendon. "*He had a courage of the
most cleere and keene temper, and soe farre from feare
that he was not without appetite of daunger, and
therfore upon any occasyon of action he alwayes engaged his person in those troopes which he thought
by the forwardnesse of the Commanders to be most
like to be farthest engaged, and in all such encounters
he had aboute him a strange cheerefulnesse and com-
paniablenesse.*" These last words are most apt
to his case. During the 13th, when generals and
staffs were in utter perplexity as to where the
line stood, and were receiving scarcely varying
messages of disaster, the report which Francis
sent back to General Greenly was a welcome
relief. He concluded thus: "What a bloody
day! Hounds are fairly running!"

On the 16th General De Lisle addressed
the regiment. "I have to congratulate your
squadron as usual," he told Francis. "I hope
you will tell the men how very grateful and
proud I am of the way they helped me to hold
the line." The Ninth were given two days' rest,

and on 18th May moved again into the Salient. There they remained in support till the night of Sunday the 23rd, when they took over the front line from the 15th and 19th Hussars at Hooge. Colonel Beale-Browne had under his command, in addition to the Ninth, 400 of the Yorkshire Regiment and 120 of the Durham Light Infantry. His front was divided into two sections—the right being held by " A " Squadron under Captain Noel Edwards, with 120 Yorkshires and 120 Durhams ; the left by " B " Squadron under Francis, with the two regimental machine guns and about 200 Yorkshires. " C " Squadron, under Rex Benson, was in support. Raymond Greene, acting as second-in-command, was in general charge of the left section.

On the morning of Sunday the 23rd Francis, along with his Colonel, attended early Communion. I have said little of that religion which was so strong a feature of his character, for it was of the simple and vital type which is revealed more in deeds than in phrases. He was never at ease in Sion, and shunned the professions of facile piety. But he did not lose his childlike trust in God, and drew strong and abiding comfort from a creed which was as forthright and unquestioning as a mediæval crusader's. He and Rivy during their brief campaign together read the 121st Psalm every morning. Francis never went into a match, much less a battle, without prayer. For men like Bishop Furse he had a profound regard, and whenever he got the chance would bring him to talk to his squadron. His Colonel, who knew him in those last hours when men's hearts are bared, has borne witness how much his religion meant to him.

The dawn of Monday, 24th May, promised a perfect summer day with cloudless skies and a light north-easterly breeze. About three a.m. the cavalry in the trenches saw a thick yellow haze, thirty feet high, rolling down from the ridge a hundred yards before them, and the air was filled with a curious pungent smell. They had had no previous experience of gas, and in twenty seconds the cloud was upon them. Then came the German guns, making a barrage behind to keep back reinforcements. Though our respirators at the time were elementary the cavalry managed to weather the gas, and held their ground through the seventeen long hours of daylight that followed. It was the last phase of the battle, and the German assault broke for good on that splendid steadfastness.

But a high price was paid for victory. In the small hours of the 25th a little party of some forty men stumbled in the half light along the Menin road, through the crumbling streets of Ypres, and out into the open country towards Vlamertinghe. Those who passed them saw figures like spectres, clothes caked with dirt, faces yellow from the poison gas. They were all that remained of the 9th Lancers. Their Brigadier, General Mullens, met them on the road, but dared not trust himself to speak to them. " Tell them," he told the Colonel, " that no words of mine can express my reverence for the Ninth." Next day General Byng, who commanded the Cavalry Corps, visited the remnant. " Put anything in orders you like," he said. " Nothing you can say will be adequate to my feelings for the old Ninth. Of course I knew you would stick it, but that doesn't lessen my unbounded admiration of you all."

With them they brought the body of Francis Grenfell. When the attack opened and the infantry on the left fell back, he was busy converting a communication trench into a fire trench, and shouting out in his old cheery way, " Who's afraid of a few dashed Huns ? " He stood on rising ground behind the trench when he was shot through the back. He managed to send a message to his squadron, the true testament of the regimental officer : " Tell them I died happy, loving them all." Then he who had once lived cheerfully in the sun, but for months had been among the fogs and shadows, went back to the sunlight.

He was buried in the churchyard of Vlamer-tinghe, and beside him was laid Sergeant Hussey, one of the most gallant N.C.O.'s in the Ninth. Some one said at the graveside, " How happy old Hussey would have been to know he died with Francis."

I have quoted already from Clarendon's character of Falkland, and if it be permitted to construe knowledge in terms not of academic learning but of self-understanding and self-mastery, the closing words of the tribute to the young Marcellus of the Civil War may be Francis's epitaph : " *Thus fell that incomparable younge man in the fowre-and-thirtieth yeere of his Age, havinge so much dispatched the businesse of life that the oldest rarely attayne to that immense knowledge, and the youngest enter not into the world with more innocence. Whosoever leads such a life neede not care upon how shorte a warninge it be taken from him.*"

INDEX.

THE END.

PRINTED IN GREAT BRITAIN AT
THE PRESS OF THE PUBLISHERS.